The Leopard in the Pool

The Leopard
in the Pool

Pat Sankar and Linda Ricard

Copyright © 2010 by The Spirit of Compassion.

Library of Congress Control Number: 2010916101
ISBN: Hardcover   978-1-4568-0460-2
               Softcover   978-1-4568-0459-6
               Ebook   978-1-4568-0461-9

This book was printed in the United States of America.

To order additional copies of this book, contact:
Xlibris Corporation
1-888-795-4274
www.Xlibris.com
Orders@Xlibris.com
88507

Dedicated to Bhagavan Sri Sathya Sai Baba

This book is also dedicated to all of those who question their existence and purpose on earth and who are ready to end the chapter of their one-dimensional lives full of accomplishments, experiences, and memories to embark on an entirely new, multi-dimensional chapter of self-discovery and spirituality.

Acknowledgments

I am grateful to so many people for making this book possible. First of all, I offer my sincere gratitude for everything I have learned at the feet of the masters too numerous to mention, too generous to appropriately respond to in gratitude, and too sublime to comprehend. I have been inspired beyond imagination by the life and teachings of Sri Sathya Sai Baba, my dearest friend, philosopher, guide and God; by the incredible life of Jesus Christ; the blemishless compassion of Buddha, the extraordinary wisdom and playfulness of Sri Krishna; the inimitable example of Sri Rama; the lectures of Swami Vivekananda; the gospel of Sri Ramakrishna; the sublime wisdom of Sri Ramana Maharishi; the authentic wisdom of Shri Shankaracharya; the tantalizing challenge of Nisargadatta Maharaj; the unforgettable autobiography of Yogananda; the practical wisdom of Robert Adams; the fountain of the source of knowledge of Atmananda Krishna Menon; the amazing series of books on conversations with God by Neal Donald Walsh; *The Power of Now* by Eckhart Tolle; the dearest members of my family; my close-knit circle of friends and fellow pilgrims; my numerous coworkers and even casual acquaintances—as you can see, the list goes on and on. This list can never be complete, since life itself is a school and we are all simultaneously students and teachers; we learn from each other, and, in turn, we teach each other. We learn what to do from others who set good examples, and learn what not to do from those who set "not so good" examples. Nevertheless, we are learning all the time and learning from everyone. Most important, nature is teaching us in abundance how to live life selflessly.

My special gratitude goes to my co-author, Linda Ricard, without whose active participation, encouragement, and rewriting of significant portions, this book would not have taken shape in its present form. Linda brought her years of experience as a speechwriter and communications specialist into full force to help me with this book.

Last but not least, I am grateful to Zoë Rosenfeld for her patience, insight, and thoughtful comments, which enhanced this book significantly despite the limited time she had to review the book.

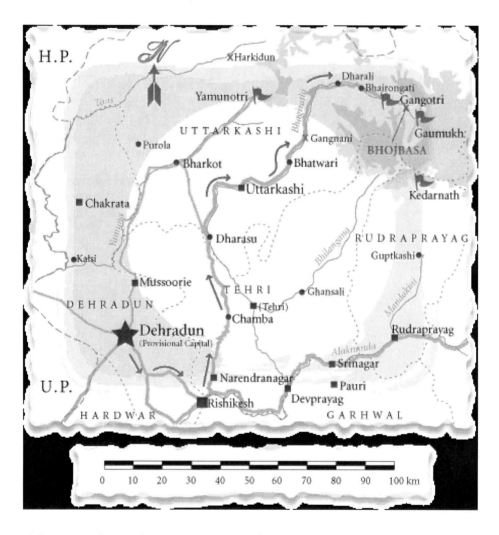

This map shows the area around Rishikesh, Gangotri, and Gomukh in North India, as well as other nearby places.

Chapter 1

Vivek Venki Venkataraman stared intently through the floor-to-ceiling glass window of his Manhattan office at the sea of headlights on the streets 50 stories below. It was 11:00 p.m. and the city still sizzled with energy. Normally he would have left for home hours ago. But today was different. There was no one in the office except him. His cup of Starbucks had gotten cold, and a residue of cream floated on its dark surface. Vivek was lost in the labyrinth of his thoughts. At 35, he already felt as if he were facing the onset of a midlife crisis. He was physically exhausted and deeply drained. It seemed to him he had already lived a full life, with a series of accomplishments, accolades, and job titles, and a sports car and a condo on Fifth Avenue to go along with all the rest. He had achieved the American dream, at least on paper, yet he couldn't shake the feeling of being empty inside. He started pacing nervously in front of the large window, his silhouette looming large on the pane of glass.

Vivek had graduated summa cum laude from Harvard with an MBA and had gone on to become a very successful businessman. He had made millions and lost millions, but he made sure that he made more than he lost. He was surrounded by everything he could dream of—money, power, and approval—yet in the end all of it had merely left him disillusioned and depressed. Vivek paced furiously, balling his fists. "I have to get away," he said to himself. This was his last day at work.

He had decided a few months earlier that he would learn more about New Age spirituality. He'd bought books, attended seminars, surfed the Internet, and religiously watched Oprah Winfrey and Dr. Phil. After sifting through the onslaught of wisdom, spiritual guidance, and advice, he'd zeroed in on a teacher whom he felt held the panacea he was seeking: Guru Swami Satpurushananda at Rishikesh[1] in India. Vivek was impressed by the stature of the guru and liked what he had heard from many of the guru's followers and from neutral observers. Here was a serious teacher willing to show the way. Vivek had decided that he would become Swami Satpurushananda's disciple. He knew that he would have to live in the Swami's ashram[2] in India to undergo his spiritual training, and he felt ready to begin.

Vivek turned away from the window and walked back to his desk. He had told a few people at work that he was leaving, but not his parents, for though he knew they would worry about him, he didn't want them to try to dissuade him from his journey. He took one final glance at his computer screen before shutting it down. He gathered his things and walked to the door. Turning around one last time, he shut off the lights and walked away from the life he had known and all that was familiar.

Hours later, he boarded a flight to India from John F. Kennedy Airport. As the jet engines roared for takeoff and the plane sailed down the runway, he mulled over his brief but eventful life. He wanted to forget his childhood, a time of loneliness and longing, as his parents had been too busy working and molding a lifestyle to teach him about the real meaning of life and his importance in it. Vivek was an introvert, and although outwardly he could successfully mingle with people, appear funny, and even inspire them, deep down, he was a lonely man. Strange as it may seem, though he chose to be lonely he was also afraid of being alone.

This was the first time that Vivek had ever done anything impulsive in his entire life. Everything always had to be analyzed before he made a decision. Vivek laughed to himself, "I am leaving everything that meant a lot to me, in search of something I do not even have the vaguest idea about." As the plane broke through the clouds and gained altitude, he settled comfortably into his seat. He began to nod off and was in a deep slumber when the

---

[1]   Rishikesh: The sacred valley just before the Ganges enters the plains of India. In Sanskrit, this word means "the place where one can master the senses."

[2]   Ashram: A hermitage where a guru or spiritual teacher lives with his students. An ashram can also be considered as an in-residence spiritual school.

snack cart came around an hour later. Vivek was soon well on his maiden journey to the Himalayas, the natural breeding place for gurus—the spiritual teachers who guide one to finding the truth within.

The long journey was almost uneventful; he slept through nearly all of it. When he arrived, he went to his hotel and checked in for his short stay—he was only planning to be in Delhi for a couple of days before heading north east. He had not been to Delhi, or to India at all, for that matter, in quite a few years, and it was always a new experience for Vivek to land in a country of billion people. He felt as if the entire population of Delhi were squeezed into Chandini Chowk, one of the popular shopping centers. This time, however, he was hardly distracted by the sights and smells of Delhi, as he was a man on a mission, bent on getting to Rishikesh and to Swami Satpurushananda's ashram.

When Vivek got to Rishikesh with nothing more than his backpack, he had no idea what was in store for him. He was brimming with enthusiasm, full of expectations and an imagined sense of relief that finally he had come to a place of peace, his own Shangri-la, a La La Land of uninterrupted bliss.

The modest Himalayan ashram was situated on the banks of the holy river Ganges at Rishikesh. Since he arrived late in the day, he had a quick supper of roti, some rice and dhal, and retired for the night in a bare room furnished with just a cot, some towels, and a bath. He got up early the next morning anxious for a glimpse of Swami Satpurushanandji. When he arrived at the prayer hall, it was overflowing with other early birds who had arrived there for the same reason.

At 8:00 a.m., Swami Satpurushananda arrived. He was a tall, well-built man with a flowing beard and a charming smile. Behind the social exterior was a distant look that could make anyone nervous to take liberties with him while talking. He took his position cross-legged on a mat on a raised platform. The day's chanting began and continued for almost two hours.

Vivek was not used to sitting through long hours of prayer or meditation. Accustomed to the rapid decision-making model driving corporate America and to endless to-do lists, as well as to living perpetually in the analytical part of his brain, Vivek felt meditation seemed like a goal that he couldn't quite reach. Just when he thought he had settled his mind to meditate, another seemingly random thought would pop up. He tried shutting off the valve of ideas, thoughts, and emotions, but the more he tried, the more of an avalanche effect it had. Shaking off the habits of Western living was harder to do than he had anticipated. His internal frustration continually overrode his internal peace. His legs cramped at times and he longed to stretch them. His back ached from sitting stationary for so long. Finally, after what seemed like an eternity, the chanting stopped. Vivek let out a sigh of relief that was nearly inaudible so as to not alert the pious devotees around him. There were melodious songs in Hindi and in Sanskrit, and then, at the end, there was Aarathi, when a priest waved a huge lamp with burning camphor in front of the statues of Hindu gods, as well toward Satpurushanandji. The guru graciously accepted all these adorations with his hands raised in a benedictory posture. He talked to a few selected devotees out of a long line waiting for the coveted chance to speak with the teacher. To Vivek, it appeared as a random process—Satpurushanandji choosing to speak with some while seemingly ignoring others.

Satpurushanandji hardly took notice of Vivek. The devotees of Satpurushanandji, however, did notice and conversed about him in hushed tones and averted eyes. He gathered that from his accent and demeanor, they were speculating that he was a wealthy American, and they clearly wondered what had brought him to the ashram. A father in the crowd with several daughters to marry off even seemed to think that Vivek would be an ideal candidate for a son-in-law. Nonetheless, the guru continued to meditate and, at times, talk to others, but not to Vivek, whom he ignored for the next five days.

As they days passed, Vivek grew more and more frustrated. He was used to special treatment and didn't know how to handle being ignored. On the sixth day, he was summoned by the guru. Feeling a bit anxious, he approached, but before he could formally introduce himself, Satpurushanandji raised his hands and stopped him, saying, "Yes, I know. You have come from America. You are dissatisfied with your life. I did not talk to you before because I was waiting for an auspicious time. You came six days before Navarathri. Today is the first day of nine nights devoted to the celebration in the name of the Divine Mother seeking inner wisdom. With mother's blessings, your ignorance will melt away. What is it you want from me?"

Vivek replied, "Sir, I have decided to become your student. Please tell me, what is the internship like here in your ashram? What is the curriculum? Who will be my instructors and what are their credentials?" Vivek's brain mentally began processing all of the tasks and information needed to kick off his spiritual itinerary. In his Western way of thinking, time was money and time wasted was not a return on investment.

Satpurushanandji remained unperturbed. "What do you mean by 'internship'?" he asked. Vivek replied, "Guruji, in Western civilization, an internship is where someone is trained by or is an apprentice under an expert."

The Guruji nodded. "Oh! In that case we offer a forty-year internship for everyone who wants to become a disciple."

Vivek couldn't believe what he was hearing, "What? Forty years?"

Satpurushanandji went on, "An internship here takes forty years. For the first ten years, the disciple masters his body and becomes a karma yogi; for the next ten years he masters his mind to become a raja yogi; and ten years after that, he develops his heart to control his feelings to become a bhakthi yogi. During the final ten years, he refines his intellect to seek the truth to become a jnana yogi."

Vivek was stunned by what he had just heard. "What, a forty-year internship? In forty years I'll be seventy-five years old—or even dead, for that matter," he thought. "For heaven's sake, it doesn't even take someone forty years to become a doctor or a lawyer."

Simultaneously annoyed at the length of a spiritual education and intrigued by the possibilities, Vivek carefully sought to balance his emotions. He was itching to know what he would be doing for the first ten years of his spiritual education. He secretly wished that he could somehow accelerate the process and master all the requirements to become a disciple and graduate early. His brain kept processing all of the possibilities.

When Vivek asked Satpurushanandji about what exactly this karma yoga[3] training during the first ten years meant, Satpurushanandji replied, "During the first ten years you do nothing but stay and help in the kitchen. You wash the rice and cook it. You peel the potatoes, hundreds of them, morning and evening, and cut the beans. You then clean the kitchen floor and the ashram bathrooms. When you have spare time, you go to the garden and tend to the flowers and the plants."

Vivek could feel his shock registering on his face. He couldn't envision himself peeling potatoes and cleaning bathrooms for ten years. He persisted in his questions. "But what about darshan, the study of scriptures, and personal time with you?"

Satpurushanandji looked at Vivek, mildly irritated at the nature of his questioning. He didn't blink as he answered, "Not for the first ten years. In fact, you won't see me that much. It is just work, work and more work, until you master the attitude towards working. Most people view work as a burden; as the biggest obstacle towards happiness. Work is worship, and the only way to realize that is to work and do more work, until it becomes second nature. No one can remain lazy and hope to obtain enlightenment. *Idam sariram parobakhaaram.* This body is to be primarily used for service to others, and not indulged in narcissistic activities like pleasure."

Vivek gulped before launching into his next question. "Guruji, I can understand how a forty-year internship would work for a normal student, but what about advanced disciples who can rapidly grasp the concepts and principles? Can't you make an exception and develop an accelerated program for these students?"

Satpurushanandji continued to stare back, unblinking. His exceedingly calm demeanor unnerved Vivek, who was used to always being on top of his game. "Young man, in this ashram we do not negotiate or barter. The rules are the same for everyone. It seems to me that the rigor of the ashram may be a little too much for you. In that case I suggest that you become a devotee if you are so inclined. These devotees are a strange bunch."

---

3   Karma Yoga: The yoga of action. The Sanskrit word "yoga" refers to perfection or excellence in chosen path. Karma yoga refers to perfection or excellence in action.

"They come and leave when they please. If their prayers are answered, they praise me to the sky. If their wishes are not fulfilled, they put me down and talk ill of me. Once again, when things turn for the better, they come again and offer to break a hundred and eight coconuts[4]. I am just a witness to all these demonstrations of devotion. You are always welcome to come and see me and practice the teachings at your own leisure. However, I hold my disciples to a very high standard of self-discipline and perseverance."

Vivek was a bit insulted and slighted by Swami Satpurushananda's rebuke. He felt like a puppy that had been nipped at by an older dog. He quickly regained his composure, and undaunted, launched into a personal question. "So, if your students are busy all day working for forty years, then sir, what do you do during the day?"

Satpurushanandji replied, "Well, that is easy to answer. I have become old and infirm. Hence my activities are limited. I get up at 5:30 a.m. and do my prayers after morning ablutions. I drink a cup of buttermilk, and I come here and sit for darshan. Streams of visitors come. I talk to some of them if I feel that they need my help. At 11:00 a.m. I take my lunch—a couple of chapthis, dhal and a little bit of curd rice. Then I retire and rest for a couple of hours, mostly to give the ashramites some free time. I come back here at 4:00 p.m. and give darshan until 7:00 p.m. before I retire for the night. On special festival days I give a discourse expounding the greatness of God, whether the devotees listen to me or not. Each day is a just a mere repetition of the previous day. This is how I lead my life. Why did you want to know?" His unwavering gaze gave way to an upturned eyebrow.

Vivek's one strength, which was also his greatest weakness, became apparent in his next question: "I also want to be a guru. I feel that I have what it takes to be one. So I'm not sure that I would need to go through an entire forty-year internship. In fact, I don't even think that I would need to enroll

---

[4]   It is customary in India for a devotee to break a hundred and eight coconuts as a sacrifice to their chosen deity if a prayer is fulfilled. The breaking of the coconut symbolizes surrender, since the hard shell represents the ego and the soft inner core the moist heart filled with devotion. The hard outer shell is discarded, and the soft inner core is distributed to everyone.

as a disciple. I could easily carry out your duties, manage the ashram and take it to new heights. I would like to be your successor." Patience was not his greatest virtue.

Satpurushanandji sighed and shook his head in disappointment. Vivek's arrogance, narcissism and pride were instantly replaced with humility and apprehension. "This is precisely the problem of the modern man," Satpurushanandji said, "Instant gratification and narcissism. We want to be instant gurus and world-class teachers, even though we may not possess the needed knowledge and experience to become one. Spirituality is not something you just attain overnight or through a class certificate or seminar. Instant gratification is linked to the ego and worldly success. Spirituality is not about instant gratification, young man." He went on, "Human birth is a great gift. The human body and the human intellect are gifts and amazing miracles of the divine. They are not meant to be misused for money or material possessions or for climbing the career ladder."

Satpurushanandji then turned away from Vivek, signaling that the dialogue had ended. From that point on, he ignored Vivek altogether, not giving him the time of day. With his tail between his legs and carrying his bruised ego along with his luggage, Vivek departed from the ashram and headed for Delhi. On the trek back, he kept wondering how it had all gone so irrevocably wrong and how he could have flunked Spirituality 101.

Chapter 2

Vivek left the austerity of the ashram to enjoy the comforts of a five-star resort in Delhi. The day after he checked in, he decided to relax and enjoy some masala tea in one of the resort's restaurants. As he leisurely sipped the tea and settled back into the comfort of a padded armchair, he couldn't help but replay his conversation with Satpurushanandji at the ashram in his mind. In the end, he came to the conclusion that although one spiritual door had just slammed shut in his face, perhaps another would open to fulfill his dream of becoming a guru. His gaze wandered aimlessly around the room. Suddenly he was caught off-guard by a large poster that read "How to Become a Guru in One Day." Vivek sat upright and stared at the picture of a handsome man in his fifties whom he surmised to be the guru.

Intrigued, he set his tea down, walked across the room and put on his reading glasses. Vivek could not believe what he read:

Do not miss this unique opportunity to meet his holiness Vimalananda, the teacher who trains gurus by the thousands. You too can become a New Age guru.

In small letters it read "Basic workshop $1,000 (U.S. dollars). For more information, contact Deepa at 91723-456-7800."

There were commendations about the workshop from the *New York Times* and *India Abroad.* Vivek could feel his adrenaline pumping. This was exactly what he needed.

Vivek pulled out his cell phone and immediately began dialing Deepa. She invited him to her office, which happened to be located just down the street from the resort.

As Vivek entered Deepa Agarwal's office, she walked over and shook his hand. Vivek could feel her taking note of his tailored slacks, silk shirt, custom shoes, diamond graduation ring, and Rolex watch, and could see that she assumed he was a man of money. After he explained to her that he was interested in attending the workshop, she walked back to her desk, motioned for Vivek to have a seat, and started looking at her computer screen. After a number of clicks, she looked at Vivek apologetically and said, "I'm sorry, Vivek, the workshop is completely booked. Our total capacity is 480, and at this point, we're overbooked by almost 20 people. We are hoping that some attendees might not show up. I wish you had contacted me yesterday. This is actually one of the most popular spiritual workshops in India. Attendees come from all countries and continents around the world."

Vivek felt like another bubble had burst. He had now been rejected twice in a few days and was not used to this feeling of disappointment. Accomplishments, achievements and accolades had always come easily to him. He summoned up the last vestiges of persistence and tenacity and shifted in his seat while strategizing his next move, as if it were a game of chess. He leaned forward and stared into Deepa's eyes, "You don't understand," he said, "I have to attend this workshop. Tell me what it will take to get me in . . . please. If not today, then when can I attend?"

Deepa rolled her eyes and flashed a smile. "Sir Guruji is very busy. After this morning's session, he is flying to Kuala Lumpur to conduct a workshop in the morning. Then he's off to Tokyo, Amsterdam, and New York, among other cities. He will not be back in Delhi for another three months. We have not scheduled that far in advance yet. However, if you leave your name and number, I will let you know when his next workshop is here in Delhi."

Vivek started to get frustrated and quickly decided to turn it back into persistence. Grabbing a wad of money from his pocket, he told Deepa, "Please. I would really like to attend this workshop. Money is no object." He held out the money to her. "I have $2,000. Please get me in. I will even stand in the farthest corner of the room if I have to. I have to hear Guruji."

Of course, who can underestimate the power of Lakshmi[5], whether she deals in Indian rupees or U.S. dollars. Deepa hesitated and bit her lip as she tried to come up with a solution. Shaking her head, she turned back and shuffled through her computer files. After a minute of awkward silence as she read the information on the screen and jotted down notes on a pad of paper, she leaned back in her chair with a smile. "Mr. Vivek," she said. "You are in luck, or should I say, you are a lucky man. A couple of participants have just dropped out of the workshop. I can squeeze you in. Welcome aboard. The workshop starts in twenty minutes. You had better get going if you're going to make it." Vivek excitedly handed over his money and shook her hand. "Thank you! This day is now the beginning of the rest of my life." Deepa smiled knowingly back at him and watched him as he hurried out her office.

Twenty minutes later, Vivek walked back into the five-star resort he was staying in and continued down a long hallway until he came to the grand ballroom hosting the conference. He anxiously entered the overcrowded ballroom and noticed that every seat was taken. People stood along the walls and congregated at the back while a sense of exhilarated energy undulated around the room. Vivek looked around the room and wondered what had drawn the other participants to the workshop. Perhaps they were IT geeks who couldn't find life's meaning in software applications, or millionaires who weren't content with their wealth, or perhaps financiers who had lost heavily in the recent stock-market crash and who were grasping for some semblance of hope and optimism in a down economy. Whatever the reason, each had a story to tell and a story to build about their life's journey and what had brought them together for this event.

A fever of whispers echoed around the room and abruptly abated when Deepa walked onstage with the handsome, middle-aged man Vivek had seen earlier on the poster. Vivek was surprised to see Deepa so soon after their conversation in her office. He was impressed with the guru's appearance, air of confidence, and authoritative demeanor.

As hushed voices drifted into silence, the Guruji spoke in a majestic and pleasing voice. "Brothers and sisters, welcome to our workshop on how to

---

5   Lakshmi: Goddess of wealth, one among the trinity who protects the entire creation.

become a guru in one day. You can become whatever you want to become. It gives me great pleasure to meet you all in person. However, I have to inform you that I will not be staying long. I will have to depart for the airport in a couple of minutes. But all I need is one PowerPoint slide to show you how to become a guru, and then it is all left up to your ingenuity."

What? Guruji was not going to spend the whole day there as advertised? The crowd gasped. Guruji continued, "The first lesson to learn is in the beauty of the simplicity of life. For example, water flowing freely is a simple act of nature. It flows in the path of least resistance. We can learn a lot from water. Now if you look at the slide on the screen, you'll see five simple phrases. That, my friends, is all you need to learn to become a guru. All you have to do is memorize these phrases. My trusted assistant Deepa will demonstrate to you how this works. Now I must be on my way to the airport. Hope to see some of you in the advanced workshop."

The guru had come, had spoken, had shown one PowerPoint slide and was gone. The crowd was left speechless as they read the messages on the slide:

"I see how you might think this way.
I know.
I understand how you feel.
Wise choice.
Sure."

Vivek felt all the others recoiling along with him as they did the math in their heads. They had just dished out $1,000 for five affirmations. That was all you needed to learn to become a guru? This couldn't be true. This was starting to look more like a New Age therapy session than an educational forum on enlightened spiritual development. Audience members began to shift uncomfortably in their seats as the realization that they had been scammed began to hit home.

Deepa came back and ensured everybody that the Guruji's teachings would be demonstrated for everyone to see for themselves. She asked for a volunteer. Vivek looked around the room to see who raised their hand. Seeing no one jumping out of their seat, he turned back and waved his hand in the air. Deepa smiled and beckoned him toward the stage. Off to the side, she whispered instructions to him on what to do once he got onstage, which struck him as a bit absurd, but he decided to play along. Deepa then turned to the audience and said, "Mr. Vivek Venkataraman will demonstrate how this works."

They ushered in an audience member who had been waiting in the wings while Vivek, wearing a fake turban, sat in a meditative posture on a divan at the center of the stage. He read over his script while the audience member read over his as he entered the stage and approached him.

Devotee: "Guruji, my life is a mess."
Vivek: "I see how you might think this way."
Devotee: "I have no peace of mind."
Vivek: "I understand how you feel."
Devotee: "I think I need to change my ways."
Vivek: "Wise choice."
Devotee: "I need your blessings to start my life anew."
Vivek: "Sure."

The interview was then over and the devotee was guided off of the stage as another one entered stage right and approached Vivek.

Devotee: "Guruji, life is hard!"
Vivek: "I see how you might think this way."
Devotee: "I stress about things day and night."
Vivek: "I know."
Devotee: "Maybe I need to do something differently in order to have different results."
Vivek: "Wise choice."
Devotee: "I would like your blessings to start my life with a clean slate."
Vivek: "Sure."

The same scenario repeated again with yet another devotee, but this time Vivek cleverly mixed up all of the affirmations as prompted in his script.

Devotee: "Guruji, why is it that my life is so full of challenges and obstacles? Why can't things go right for once?"
Vivek: "I know."

Devotee: "I'm tired of thinking, strategizing and analyzing every decision I make. I just want some peace in my life. I don't want to have to think all of the time. I just want to exist . . . to be."

Vivek: "I understand how you feel."

Devotee: "Maybe instead of wanting the things around me to change, I should change something in my life to make it better."

Vivek: "Wise choice."

Devotee: "I ask your blessings to jumpstart my life again."

Vivek: "Sure."

The audience cheered loudly over the power of the five affirmations, but Vivek didn't share the group's enthusiasm. He felt cheated and frustrated and decided not to waste any more of his valuable time. He could see where this was going and he had no intention of going along with it. At the break, he made his exit, leaving behind the gullible audience members lured by monetary gain, who seemed to him like sheep blindly following a shepherd into a den of wolves. Vivek left the workshop bitterly disappointed, disillusioned, and disheartened.

Chapter 3

Vivek had failed miserably in his two initial attempts at becoming a guru. First, Swami Satpurushananda in his Himalayan ashram had condemned him to forty years of internship and proceeded to ignore him, and then he felt sick over cheating gullible people with clever phrases on stage in a fraud of a workshop. What a waste of his money, time, and effort. He realized in retrospect that Vimalananda and Deepa Agarwal were only scam artists with no ounce of spirituality in them. They only worshipped the source of all grief, anger, and greed: the almighty dollar. As disgusted as he was with the false pretense of spirituality presented in the workshop, Vivek still clung to the hope of discovering what becoming a guru really was all about and how that would turn his life around and create meaning where there had been only emptiness.

Vivek had spent the last few months traveling across India, visiting several cities—all the while reading avidly. Now, relaxing in his five-star hotel in Chennai, he continued to spend his time reading books and blogs on spirituality. Since setting out on his trip, he had read about Zen, read deeply about the Buddha, read esoteric texts on Jesus, and read the Patanjali Yogasutra, the Bhagavad Gita, *Conversations with God*, Eckhart Tolle, Deepak Chopra, Jack Canfield, Gregg Braden, *Autobiography of a Yogi*, talks by Vivekananda, *Himalayan Masters* by Ram Dass, and books on Ramana Maharishi, to name a few. But the more he read, the more he knew that he didn't really know anything. He knew more and more, but understood less and less.

His six-month visa was going to expire. On the last leg of his journey, he decided to visit Thiruvannamalai, a temple town located 200 miles south of Chennai in South India. He wondered, "Did Thiruvannamalai make Ramana Maharishi famous or did the Maharishi make Thiruvannamalai famous?" He stayed at the Ramanashram[6]. One day he decided on the long circumambulation—a circular walk with a reverential and prayerful attitude—of the famous hill there, supposedly filled with vibrant spiritual energy. He walked barefoot, armed with a water bottle in one hand and a rosary in the other. He did not know what to chant. He had tried so many mantras in the past, but they did not satisfy his intellectual curiosity. Besides, he felt it was stupid to talk to oneself all of the time.

Vivek started the walk at 6:30 a.m., with a cool breeze blowing lightly against his skin. By 8:00 a.m., however, the sun was out in full force and Vivek was breaking out in a sweat. He was mentally, physically, emotionally and spiritually tired: tired of searching for the meaning of his life and tired from knowing that he would have to go back to the States to his old life. He shuddered at the thought that he would be going back home defeated, empty-handed, and more ignorant than when he'd started and have to get back into the full swing of the stock market, startups, celebrity dinners, and political lobbies. Worse yet, his parents might finally convince him to marry a village girl from South India. He detested the thought of it all. "Why did my parents name me Vivek, which means 'the wise one'?'" he pondered. "I am not wise, I am actually otherwise."

He spotted an area of cool shade under a large tree a few hundred feet up the hill, away from the meandering path. He clambered up and settled himself on an uneven rock, gulping what was left in his water bottle. Wiping a dribble from his chin, he couldn't help but be reminded of a couple of idlis and vadas soaked in cup of sambar, with a bit of onion chutney to go along with steaming-hot South Indian filtered coffee. Oohh! That sounded tasty. Vivek might have been born in the U.S. to Indian parents and spoon-fed commercialism and fast food as he was Americanized over the years, but he had never overcome his yearning for the comfort of South Indian cuisine. Vivek became simultaneously frustrated with his thoughts and his stomach. He thought to himself, "Stomach, I have fed you hamburgers, the finest

---

6   Ramanashram: A spiritual hermitage at Thiruvannamalai. This hermitage was inspired by Ramana Maharishi (Great Sage) who lived sixty years ago and who revived the path of wisdom by popularizing the enquiry path of asking "Who am I?"

wine, and the fanciest cuisine that the world has to offer. Yet you are never satisfied. You always want more and more. I am tired of you. And you, brain, you are even worse. You are greedy. No matter how much I please you with the senses, you want more, more and more. I am tired of the two of you. I wish I could be free of your constant and ungrateful needs."

A voice suddenly rang out from behind a tree, "My son, do not get mad at your mind and your stomach. They are just doing their dharma[7]. The mind is supposed to think and desire all the time. The stomach is supposed to eat periodically to keep you well nourished." Startled, Vivek craned his neck to see who had spoken, and to his astonishment, saw no one. He shouted, "Who is reading my thoughts?"

A venerable sage with a childlike smile peered out from behind the tree. He laughed and his belly shook. "I did not read your thoughts," he said. "On the contrary, you came to my meditation place and disturbed me with your thoughts." The saintly person could not have been more than 70. He had a very fair complexion, unlike most of the South Indians in this area. He sported a silvery-white mustache and beard and was wearing clean clothes, a dhothi and an upper-body garment thrown over his shoulder as a shawl. Not only that, but he was speaking perfect English.

Vivek said, "Sir, I am sorry I disturbed you. I shall go somewhere else. It was just my frustration. I was deep in thought."

The sage replied, "That is okay. I do not mind your company at all. As a matter of fact, I was expecting you."

Vivek could feel himself light up with curiosity. "What?" he said. "First you read my thoughts and complain that I disturbed you. Now you're saying you were waiting for me, expecting me. Who are you really? Are you from the CIA or the FBI?" he teased. "Are you following me or something?"

---

[7]   Dharma: A common interpretation for this Sanskrit word is "duty" or "responsibility."
A deeper and more profound meaning of the word refers to a process by which an individual attains a chosen goal (ultimately, perfection itself) in life. So any act or event which delays, prevents, or derails the progress toward the goal is called adharmic or against dharma.

The wise sage giggled, "Son, not only do I belong to the CIA and FBI, but I also belong to the CBI. CBI stands for 'Constant Bliss Incarnate,' FBI for 'Freedom Beyond Imagination' and CIA for 'Constant Integrated Awareness.'"

Vivek was amused by the clever acronyms but had a hunch that the old man was up to something. He felt his American cynicism kicking in at the prospect of a scam.

The sage seemed to anticipate his thoughts. "Son, I do not want your money."

Vivek's brain started to race with the realization that the wise sage could actually read his mind. "Jeez!" he thought. "I can't hide anything from him."

The sage remained undaunted. "Don't be afraid of me. I know all about you."

Vivek was caught off-guard by the remark. His eyes widened in surprise and then narrowed slightly as he looked with suspicion at the sage. "What do you know about me?"

"I know everything about you," the sage replied. "More than you know about yourself, in fact. I know about your lonely childhood, about you graduating with flying colors, and about your initial disappointments with friends—especially of the other gender." The sage winked. Vivek took a deep breath and thought, "Oh, my God, he knows everything about me, but I know nothing about him." Vivek felt like he was on the losing side of a chess match and that he had been outwitted by an opponent who had just declared "Checkmate!" All sense of control was slipping away from him and he wasn't sure how to get it back.

The sage startled him again. "Believe me, I'm not interested in your autobiography. I am not interested in anything *from* you. I am only interested *in* you. Don't be afraid. I am not here to mislead you or put some kind of hex or voodoo magic on you. I am your friend. Whether you recognize me or not, I recognize you from several previous births. I am your friend, here to help you."

Vivek snorted in contempt and retorted angrily, "Don't lay that reincarnation stuff on me. I don't believe in living multiple lives. One life is more than enough for me and I want to live it to the fullest."

The sage replied, "Fair enough. I will bring up neither your past births nor your future ones again."

Vivek's curiosity got the better of him. "So you know the past and the future about me, too?"

The sage casually replied, "Yes, what is so strange about it? I thought you were not interested in such stuff."

"Wait a minute," Vivek objected. "That's impossible. No one can predict the future."

The sage replied matter-of-factly. "Is that so? Then what about the scientific systems that can predict earthquakes or weather patterns?"

Vivek folded his arms and said, "Well, that is different. Science is proven knowledge. That's not the same."

The sage chuckled and threw his hands into the air. "Why not? Prediction is prediction, whether it involves seeing one second into the future or one thousand years. It is indeed the same; it is seeing a future event in the reality of the present moment."

Vivek acquiesced. "Okay, fine, I see your point. But what are you really trying to tell me? What's the bottom line?"

The sage shook his head gently, grinning like the Cheshire Cat. "Always living your life for the bottom line. Problem is, the bottom line doesn't fill you up with happiness. The eternal search for the bottom line is like always running in a race that has no finish line. There is no meaning to the bottom line, only ultimate frustration." The sage ran his hand over his forehead, squinted at the undulating haze of the blistering sky and turned his attention back to Vivek, "Son, the sun is getting hotter and so are you. You are getting hungrier, and, shall I say, angrier, too, by the minute. Let's go to my office for some breakfast. My office is just up the hill from here."

Vivek was taken aback. Of course he was hungry and was craving hot idlis, vadas, sambar, chutney and filter coffee, but how did this guy know that? Curiosity got the better of him because he knew that he had to find out more about this all-knowing man. "Sure," he said, and began following the sage up the hill through the bushes and snake hills.

Shortly into their hike, Vivek started puffing and sweating. He could not keep pace with the rapidly climbing agile old man, who had the stamina of a 20-year-old. Vivek gasped, "Sir, can I ask you something?"

The sage replied without missing a beat or a breath, "Not now, son . . . after you eat your breakfast."

They finally reached the holy man's office after twenty minutes' brisk climb. Vivek stooped over and clutched his knees, trying to regain his strength and to calm his rapidly beating heart, which reverberated in his ears. After the much-needed oxygen silenced his labored breathing and his heart reestablished a routine cadence again, Vivek regained his composure and took a look around to assess his surroundings. Much to his surprise, instead of a steel-supported, glass enclosed office building housing frenetic professionals and their clients, what stood in front of him was simply a small cave carved into the hillside, offering just enough shelter from the rain and the heat of the sun. There was nothing in the modest dwelling except a small, burning lamp and an incense stick next to it that was still smoldering. There was also an earthen pot with a lid that Vivek assumed held water for the parched souls who braved the elements to hike up the steep hillside.

The sage motioned for Vivek to sit on the bare ground. He then extended his palm and raised it into the air. Startled, Vivek fell back as a plate full of hot rice cakes, vadas (rice and lentil pancakes), lentil soup, and chutney magically appeared out of thin air. Vivek's jaw dropped and he couldn't believe what he was seeing. He rubbed his eyes and opened them again as if expecting the plate not to be there. But it was and he was not hallucinating. In a flash, the sage also materialized a silver tumbler with steaming filter-coffee, "Enjoy the fruits of my hospitality." He then apologized, "Oh, I am sorry. I forgot a spoon. Can you eat Indian style with your fingers?" Before he finished his sentence, a famished Vivek was already digging into the idli, hungrily licking his fingers in the process. After he devoured his breakfast, he washed his hands with the water from the earthen pot and drank a little bit too. It might not have been sterilized commercial bottled water, but it was the best water he had ever drunk. He patted his stomach for reassurance and let out a luxurious sigh of contentment.

A cool breeze caressed his face, which was beaded with sweat. The trees swayed gently in the breeze, their branches lazily undulating as if dancing in the wind and their leaves rustling in response. After a moment of peaceful silence and contemplation, the sage quietly asked, "Son, what did you want to ask?"

Vivek looked over at him. "First of all, what do I call you? Guruji?" The sage grinned, "No, I am nobody's guru. You can simply call me Chidanand."

"OK, then, I will call you Chidanandji. You say you know the past and the future. If that's the case, then life must be pretty dull for you. The element of surprise is what's exciting. Predictability is boring. Am I correct?"

Chidanandji replied, "Son, on the contrary. Life is vibrant for me. I always live in the present moment, hence there is no need for me to dwell either on the past or on the future. I am perfectly satisfied and content. I accept God's will completely. The past and the future are of no use to me. Only occasionally I use my ability to impress upon rationally-minded doubting Thomases like you who have forgotten the simple art of living in the present."

Vivek objected. "Chidanandji, that may make sense for you, but not for me. You may want to sit here all day living in the present in this cave meditating on who knows what, but I'm a guy who needs a strategy, a plan that drives my goals and future results. That's what makes the corporate world go round. And why not learn from the past? It doesn't make sense if you don't learn from past mistakes to make better decisions in the present and the future. And what about our achievements, which also reside in the past and which help build our professional portfolio and our standing in society and in social networks? Personally speaking, Chidanandji, I would go bananas if I had to continually live in the present. It's not exciting enough to keep me going. It's the future that motivates me."

Chidanandji leaned over and supported his weight on his elbow. "Son, I hate to tell you this, but you're not normal now, and on top of that, you're already going bananas with your planning, strategizing, cursing, and celebrating successes—all of which, by the way, are only temporary. The only way to fully enjoy life is to live in the present, or shall we say, in the presence."

Vivek retorted, "In the presence of what? Or should I say who? God? I don't even know who God is, and frankly, I don't care. Nobody watches over me. I take care of myself."

Chidanandji gently chided him. "How you jump to conclusions! Who said anything about God? I'm talking awareness." Then he added, "And by the way, somebody *is* watching you all the time."

Vivek threw Chidanandji a skeptical look and sat upright. "*Right*, and who might that be, huh?"

Chidanandji simply replied, "Your own awareness is watching you all the time."

Vivek laughed. "Oh, I see, I watch over myself. Well, that *does* make sense. Wait a minute, does that mean that a squirrel's awareness is watching it as it runs around searching for food?"

Chidanandji continued on, unfazed by Vivek's reaction. "There is only one true awareness and it's not of the mind, but of the soul. It is like this: There is only one space. But we partition it and call it different names: houses, bodies, fields, zones, etc. Similarly, awareness is one, but focused on a limited range, it seems limited and separate. For example, you see a row of street lamps. There is light in the vicinity of the lamp and gradually becomes darkness until the region of the light from the next street lamp takes over. The light in principle is the same, but the location and the feebleness or strength of the light makes it look different."

Vivek nodded. "I get it. I like the street lamp analogy. But the question remains: Why are you telling me this? What's in it for me?"

Chidanandji gazed steadily back at Vivek, unperturbed by his skepticism. "Again, this bottom-line and 'what's in it for me' attitude. Son, did you forget that you had wanted to become an instant guru? Were you not disappointed with the Himalayan guru who imposed a forty-year internship on you? Were you not fed up with the catchy phrases taught by Vimalananda, another lost soul who has lost his way in life after being lured in by false promises of money and success?" Vivek's jaw dropped for a second time as he realized that this complete stranger knew everything about him—where he had been, who had talked to, and why he had chosen to pursue this path in his search for life's meaning. Chidanandji continued, undaunted by Vivek's reaction of shock and disbelief. "Son, I'm here to tell you that you can still instantly become a guru, but not by false pretenses and catchy phrases. The answer and methodology is already within you. You just haven't been able to find it because you've been distracted by outside influences such as money and ego gratification.

"Realization happens in an instant. You are ignorant one moment, then instantly and supremely wise. But we do not know when that instant is going to happen. It could happen right now, next month, next year, or even in the next lifetime. Oh, I forget, you don't believe in reincarnation. OK, erase that last statement."

Vivek studied Chidanandji before replying, "Yes, but what if I'm not a good enough student for realization?"

Chidanandji sat up, leaned over and reassuringly placed his hand on Vivek's arm. "Of course you are good enough. Why wouldn't you be? In fact, you're more than good enough. You could realize the truth this instant, if that were the only thing you ever wanted. But you want other things, too. You want hot idlis, sambar, chutney, filter-coffee, a comfortable place to sleep, and *also* instant realization."

Vivek decided to question Chidanandji further. "So is it wrong to like idlis? Or French fries, for that matter?"

Chidanandji was not daunted by the trick question. "Son, it is not *what* you like that is wrong. The fact *that* you like is what is wrong."

Confused, Vivek momentarily looked away, as if searching for the right question or answer. He then turned back to Chidanandji, puzzled. "Chidanandji, I'm confused. Are you telling me that my likes and dislikes are based on my thinking and that my thoughts are what are wrong?"

Chidanandji nodded, "Yes, and it didn't take your Harvard MBA to understand how your mind gets in the way of your happiness. You are right on the money. Thinking is the root cause of all the problems. Awareness, then, is the ability to know without thinking and it only happens in the present moment."

Vivek looked away and was silent for a few moments. He was trying to grasp the meaning of everything he had learned so far. He fixed his gaze back on Chidanandji. He studied the wise man's face in an attempt to organize his own thoughts. The deeply etched wrinkle lines stretched across his countenance resembled a map of intersections, routes and navigational corridors. His green eyes twinkled with wisdom and internal peace. "So, Chidanandji, how does one develop awareness?"

Chidanandji chuckled. "Vivek, you do not have to develop awareness. It is your true nature."

Vivek threw up his hands in frustration. "But I don't understand," he said.

Chidanandji continued patiently, like a father watching over his young son. "Think of it this way: We develop skills, talent and expertise. We learn to walk, talk, eat, and meditate. But you don't need to do anything to become aware. When you do nothing at all, the only thing that remains is awareness. It may take several months to become a good meditator, several years to become an accomplished musician, or several decades to become a recognized professional in your field. But I can teach you awareness in a few minutes and then you are on your own to increase your awareness of awareness."

Vivek smiled. "Awareness of awareness. I like that."

Chidanandji then guided Vivek to become aware of the various regions of his body. Vivek felt himself becoming aware of tingling sensations on the top of his head, in the center between his eyebrows, in his shoulders, his palms, the stomach region, and the soles of his feet. The energy in his palms was particularly strong and pulsating. Soon he could feel his entire body vibrating with energy. When Chidanandji stopped guiding him, he instructed Vivek to quietly sit and enjoy the waves of bliss pulsating through his body.

With the distractions of daily life erased from his mind, Vivek's senses could now detect the slightest of movement and sound. He could, for the first time in his life, discern his breathing and hear distant sounds he'd never heard before. He could even hear the sound of the bells from the yoked bullocks tied to a distant cart moving along the circular pathway 700 feet down and almost a mile away. He could detect the chirping of insects and birds as well as the rumblings of a car and a bus in the distance. The gentle breeze almost lulled him to sleep though he was fully conscious, awake and aware. After a few minutes, at the prompting of Chidanandji, Vivek opened his eyes. He had never felt so good. He had never known so much peace existed within him.

Chidanandji looked him over with curiosity. "Vivek, how do you feel?"

Vivek stretched and replied, "Wonderful! Amazing! Never felt better. Is that all there is to awareness? Wow!"

"No, son, this is just the beginning. This is the kindergarten—the nursery school of awareness. Awareness is neither a technique nor a training. It is a way of life. It is a never-ending process. Awareness is unlimited and ever increasing. First you become aware of yourself, and then you become aware of others. In the end you become aware of all of creation."

"Wow!" said Vivek. "That is phenomenal. But is it really possible?"

Chidanandji responded, "Why speculate? Why not experience?"

"But how? Just keep doing what you instructed me to do?"

Chidanandji nodded. "Yes, but you need to do that almost effortlessly, without the weight of expectation and stress or strain."

Vivek became puzzled again. "I do not understand."

Chidanandji leaned over and peered into Vivek's eyes. "Vivek, pay close attention to what I am saying. I am going to share with you many secrets of life that you normally do not hear about. I came today mainly to share this information with you. Are you ready?"

"Yes, Chidanandji, I am all ears. Please fire away."

"Vivek, normally when we meet a person, we either like or dislike him or her. This is mostly based on our assessment of their physical body, its appearance, behavior and the ability to interact with others. But a person is not just the body. He is much more than that. According to our scriptures, there are five bodies in us, like the layers of an onion.

"The first layer of your personality is your physical body, nourished by anna or food. The next layer is your breath, the next your mind, the next your intellect, and the final layer is your spiritual center, your heart. Not the physical heart, but the heart of the soul that enshrines your feelings and emotions. The negative emotions of lust, greed, and so forth are associated with the mind, and the positive, sacred emotions of truth, love, nonviolence, right action and peace are associated with the heart.

"Bodies are separate from one another and this gives rise to our distinctive personalities, as well as to our separateness from one another. Breath takes us closer. Fortunately or unfortunately, we all share the same breath or air. That is why secondary smoking causes cancer. Mind takes us even closer, as we all share the same thought field and similarly the intellect and the heartfelt emotions. Breath is subtler than the physical body, mind is subtler than the breath, intellect is subtler than the mind and the emotions (especially the sathwik emotions of compassions and ultimately love) are subtler than the intellect.

"Traditionally, what we assess to be a person is eighty percent physical, fifteen percent mental, five percent intellectual and emotional. But in reality it should be the opposite: The physical should account for only ten to twenty percent and the subtler sacred emotions eighty percent. Awareness takes you inward to become aware with your body, breath, mind, intellect, and heart to ultimately become one with universal consciousness, which is nothing but awareness minus the body, breath, mind, intellect, and heart.

"The physical body is simply a delusion of the mind which is tied to the senses and the physical world. Son, as soon as one becomes completely aware of the physical body, one transcends it. That is the key. An aspect of it is sometimes referred to as an out-of-body experience, but that is only a mere sign or indication. When you can voluntarily become fully aware of your physical body at will, then you have transcended it. Then you move on to become aware of the breath, at which point you can become aware of other physical bodies. When you transcend the breath, you start becoming aware of the mind, at which point you can perceive the pranic vibrations or aura of all. When you transcend the mind, you start becoming aware of the intellect, at which point you become aware of all minds, and the journey goes on."

Vivek blew out a breath of air. "Chidanandji, my goodness! This is a lot to digest in one sitting."

Chidanandji laughed. "And especially on a stomach loaded with rice cake, lentil soup, vadas, chutney and coffee. Son, go now to where you are staying at the Ramanashram. Rest and contemplate what we have discussed, especially about awareness. One of these days, when I think the time is right, I will reappear in your life and we can continue our discussion."

"Chidanandji," Vivek protested, "don't pique my curiosity and just disappear on me. That's not fair."

Chidanandji reached over and patted Vivek's arm. "Son, I cannot give you more than what you can digest. Information should lead to inspiration. Inspiration should lead to inner transformation." Chidanandji reassured Vivek, saying, "When you are ready for me to continue this discussion, I promise that I will come and see you."

Vivek panicked. "But Chidanandji, my six months' visa is going to expire. I have to go back to New York in a few days!"

Chidanandji shook his head and smiled at Vivek's distressed countenance. "Vivek, do you think I am limited by the seven oceans and the five continents? I *am* awareness. I am always near you, around you, above you, behind you. *Trust me.*"

Before Vivek could blink, Chidanandji disappeared into thin air. Vivek's jaw dropped for the third time that day and he looked around incredulously. Was he dreaming? No, it couldn't be, since he was still sitting on the cool dank dirt in the cave. After a few moments of muddled reflection and confusion, he pulled himself up, stretched his taut muscles, rubbed his neck and shoulders to relieve the tension born of the day's extraordinary events and started the long trek back down the hillside. Halfway down the steep incline, he fell full length on the hard ground amid rocks, thorns, and shrubs, and he sobbed, purging a lifetime of unfulfilled dreams, frustrations, and broken promises out of his heart, mind, and soul. After the negative emotions had been spent, he lay exhausted and damp with sweat, his heated cheek resting on the cooling earth. Slowly he regained his composure and got up to resume his long journey back to the Ramanashram.

Chapter 4

The jumbo jet glided across the clear sky to touch down on schedule at JFK Airport. Among the travelers making the safe passage to the U.S. from all corners of the globe was Vivek, caught up in the sea of passengers exiting the cramped quarters of the jet onto the ramp and into the busy terminal. Casually rolling his luggage behind him, he maneuvered around frustrated and distracted travelers as the sea of humanity moved him towards the exit to where a regiment of taxis waited patiently in line for customers. As he climbed into the backseat of the taxi, he gave the driver the address of his apartment and then quietly settled into his thoughts. He turned and watched a steady stream of cars racing along the freeway, like platelets traveling through the vascular system of the city, and thought back to the day of his departure from the Ramanashram.

As he was ready to leave that morning, an older man called his name and motioned to him from across the room. Vivek recognized him as the gentleman who had encouraged him the day before to trek around the hill. He approached Vivek.

"My boy," he exclaimed, "How did your hike go? Did you find it exhausting or exhilarating?" The gentleman had been told of Vivek's meeting with the Swami Chidanandji and was curious to hear the details. He didn't, however, seem to believe that there was such a person in Thiruvannamalai. After listening to Vivek's account of his extraordinary meeting with the Swami on the hilltop, he told Vivek that he had come to the conclusion that Chidanandji did not live in Thiruvannamalai, but that it must have been Lord Shiva, the God of destruction himself, who had come to Vivek.

Vivek was taken aback by this remark and could not digest the possibility of Lord Shiva appearing at Thiruvannamalai for his sake.

On the way to the airport, Vivek hadn't been able to stop thinking about Swami Chidanandji's words of wisdom and enlightenment. His entire being felt as light as air, as if a huge weight had been taken off of his back. For the first time in many years, he took notice of all of the beauty of life around him where before, in his overly critical, perfectionistic way, he had only seen the negative. Instead of grimacing at having to deal with the dirty airport, for example, he saw only the beauty of the people around him. He felt like he was walking among angels, from the ticket agents to the pilots and security guards.

It was as if he were in a state of supreme peace. He felt his serendipitous encounter with Swami Chidanandji had profoundly changed him to the core of his being. As the taxi barreled along, he felt immense gratitude for the country that had given him shelter. His gratitude extended to India for giving him his ancestral heritage and culture and to America for giving him a new life. He felt that India was his birth mother and America his foster mother. His joy at being back in New York was overwhelming and he willed the strength to contain it before tears of joy started springing from his eyes. He was bound for his home, ready to embark on his new life's trajectory.

The first month after his return to the States, Vivek struggled to adjust. He found himself wrestling with the big questions: "Who am I? Why am I here? Where do I fit in and where am I going?" He didn't feel a burning need to rejoin the rat race too soon or deal with deadlines, corporate ideology, friends' life dramas, or even world events displayed as circus characters on his high-definition flat-screen TV. Instead, he stayed home most of the time, feeling like a hermit or an introvert, trying to decide what to do. "Should I continue with retirement? Should I go back to India permanently to settle down in Rishikesh, or perhaps Thiruvannamalai? Should I retire in Hawaii? Should I get back to work? Should I get married and raise a family? What to do? What to do?"

As the months went by, he could not shake the memory of his meeting with Chidanandji. He couldn't figure out if it really was a chance meeting or not, but one thing was for sure, he really wanted to have a chance to meet with him again. But he had no idea how, when, or where that might happen, and this uncertainty left him frustrated and unsure. The fundamental question that continued to haunt him was "What is awareness and how do I live in the present?" Though he'd felt a lingering calm for a while after meeting Chidanandji, he had not been able to reproduce the ultimate peace and bliss he'd experienced in those few sacred and captured moments in time at Thiruvannamalai. He repeatedly tried to discover awareness by himself, but failed each time, leaving him more and more frustrated. He knew that something was missing and couldn't put his finger on it. Perhaps it was because he was not fully relaxed as Chidanandji had suggested.

Ultimately, he came to the conclusion that finding awareness was not a full-time job, and he began to feel he needed some other activity to keep his mind occupied, even if that meant going back to his job, at least part-time. He decided to rejoin the mass of humanity in the job market seeking to continually increase the bottom line, and go back to work as a part time senior partner in one of the investment firms. His job was to be a technical management advisor. He did not take initiatives on his own, but provided advice to other venture capital firms on their investment strategies for potential startups. As soon as he took the job, he realized that he had changed and that he couldn't get emotionally involved in the material pursuit of happiness as he had before, so he drew up a contract stating that he would only take a salary of one dollar per year and that all of his earnings would go into a trust fund that he created to help orphans, disabled children, and abandoned elders across the globe.

He talked to his long-time friend Gregory Keaton, an attorney and fellow summa cum laude graduate from Harvard, who had similar philanthropic ambitions. On the surface, one might argue that a philanthropic lawyer is simply an oxymoron and not to be taken seriously, but Greg was not one to go along with the herd, and had a mindset like that of Vivek. Greg also tried to play the game that society imposed on him. Like Vivek, he had also tried to fulfill his parents' dreams of being an academic scholar. His father was a film producer and his mother was an actress. Technically, he did not need to work but did so to relieve his guilt over not being like everyone else. Instead, he'd earned money the old-fashioned way: He'd inherited it. He was intrigued by Vivek's philanthropic dreams of giving back to humanity, and took a substantial sum of the money from his trust fund and put it into Vivek's new trust, called the Awareness Foundation, where Vivek and Greg were sole directors.

One weekend, Vivek decided to drive north to visit his parents, Dr. Ramakrishnan Venkataraman and Dr. Tripurasundari Venkataraman, who were both physicians, to discuss his new plans, his part time work, his nonprofit foundation with Greg, and his spiritual ambitions. His parents had been successful doctors in Ithaca for the better part of three decades. The doctors had been through a tumultuous time, not knowing what had happened to their son in the six months he'd been gone without even telling them where he was going. Their ears burned with gossip as news from across the continents had revealed that Vivek was suffering from a hallucination of meeting Swami Chidanandji. They wanted to make sure that he was okay and to dispel the nasty rumors that swirled around them, threatening the fabric of their family life. Their worries were replaced with relief the moment they opened the door to greet him.

Upon seeing his parents, Vivek was painfully reminded of the fact that he had always been ashamed of their accents. Although they were both naturalized citizens with an excellent command of the English language, they still harbored mild South Indian accents and Vivek never wanted his friends to hear them, lest they make fun of him. But somehow today the accents did not matter.

Vivek and his parents sat in the small living room on the lumpy couches Vivek had grown up with, a plate of fragrant masal vada (a fried lentil puff that Vivek had been fond of during his childhood days) on the coffee table. Vivek settled back and said, "I thought you guys were planning to get a new sofa set. You know, everything in here still looks the same as when I left home fifteen years ago."

His father ignored this comment, peered over his reading glasses at Vivek, and said, "Son, we were terribly worried about you! What has become of you? Your mother has not had a wink of sleep since you left. We have given you the best of everything just for this? Son, look at me when I talk to you. Respect your elders." His gazed shifted to the anxious look on his wife's face. They exchanged a glance of collaboration before launching into their well-meaning and well-rehearsed lines—lines they seemed to have talked about for months during Vivek's disappearance: "Son, your mother and I think that it is time you got married and continued the family tradition."

Although Vivek could feel his blood pressure rise and he experienced the sensation of wanting to flee from the pressure of family tradition, he remained calm and composed in his response. "Mom, Dad," he said. "I am never going to be what you want me to be. I am my own person. I've been trying to convey this to you for the last thirty-six years. I guess I have not communicated it well. Dad, I am not going to get married. Don't get me wrong—I have nothing against marriage. It is only my marriage that I am against."

His father gently chided, "Vivek! I never talked to my father that way."

His mother intervened. "What are you talking about? You never talked to your father, period." Grandpa Gopalan Ramakrishnan had been a rich landowner who'd owned multiple shops in Tanjore. He had never approved of his son's journey to America and never forgave him until his death. Though he'd accepted his grandson, he had never accepted his daughter-in-law, who had not been his first choice.

His father sighed. "Son, we are grown-up adults. Let us discuss this rationally. Why don't you want to get married?"

"Vivek, why are your torturing us?" Vivek's mother pressed. "You are our only son. I have three potential candidates for your hand. All are educated girls located here in the U.S.—one Tamilian, one Gujarathi and one Bengali. The horoscopes match. You can take your pick."

Vivek shook his head. The fact that his parent's antiquated ideas of marriage didn't align with the modern emphasis on romance was the least of the issues. "No, mom," he replied. "I do not want marriage. I do not want to ruin the lives of any of these girls."

Vivek's father's eyebrows rose in surprise. "Pardon me, is there something you want to tell us? Are you gay? Is it that Greg?"

"Come on, Dad. Get real! Honestly, I myself do not know what I want."

His father countered, "That never stopped us. Your mom and I do not know what the heck we want. But we are successful doctors, happily married and struggling with a rebellious son, it seems."

Vivek then told them in detail about his trip to India and his meeting with Chidanandji. His mother was not at all happy. "Vivek, over my dead body are you going to become a sanyasi[8]."

Vivek's father snorted. "So now you are into awareness and ready to plunge into something you have no clue about. And to think we gave you all that education and training so that you could go into the wilderness in search of awareness!"

Vivek calmly countered, "No, Dad, Mom. I am not going anywhere. I am going to continue to work part-time and work in my foundation helping needy people. But my journey into awareness is not an external journey, it is an *internal* journey."

Steaming ahead like a train at full speed, his father said, "Son, at this point, it would be easier if you were on drugs because then I could at least prescribe a treatment. I do not know how to deal with this awareness crap. But you are on your own. Do what you want, but don't come crying back to me. I am glad you are working at least part-time. As far as the foundation goes, it is a good idea." Adopting an attitude of resignation and defeat, his shoulders dropped and his gaze met the floor. "If you want, I can write you a check for a couple of million dollars." His voice was flat. "After all, it is going to come from the trust fund we established for you. Just let me know. I have to go to the hospital. Be gentle with your mother. She is going to cry and cry and drive me crazy."

After half an hour, Vivek's mother gave him a tearful send-off, insisting that he reconsider his opinion about marriage. He could tell that she'd secretly decided to continue her search for a golden bride, and felt sure that she would surreptitiously arrange a surprise meeting for him with one of these vivacious girls at a more opportune time, when it seemed to her that Vivek had come to his senses.

---

[8]   Sanyasi: A renunciant who renounces the world in search of God.

The drive back to Manhattan was a long and lonesome one for Vivek. He found himself drifting in and out of memories and thoughts as the scenery passed him by. At times he felt a longing and a tugging at his heart over hurting his parents, yet he also felt exhilarated to be taking charge of his life and not caving to archaic customs. Tired from the day's drama, he decided to stop for the night at an inn next to the freeway to rest before continuing the journey in the morning.

Vivek felt more refreshed after splashing his face with water and sitting down to a salad and fruit plate at the hotel's restaurant before he turned in for the night. He sat on his bed feeling a bit pensive and kept asking himself, "How do I develop awareness and how do I start?" He eventually fell asleep sitting up from the weight of the day's tension resting on his shoulders.

Suddenly the lights came on, and the fan started moving. He awoke with a start and looked around, only to discover that no one was there. The clock read 3:00 a.m. No longer tired after the adrenaline rush of being jolted awake, he decided to brush his teeth, take a shower, and resume his trip to New York.

Dripping wet from the shower, with a towel tied around his waist, Vivek walked aimlessly into the living room area of his hotel room, where the television, sofa, and kitchenette were. At first he couldn't see a thing because he was too busy drying his hair with a towel. Once he pulled the towel away and looked up, he yelped, "Holy crud! Don't scare me like that!" There seated on the sofa in his hotel room in full dhothi regalia was Chidanandji. The faint moonlight, making its way through the gaps in the curtains, fell on Chidanandji's chiseled face as he turned toward Vivek.

His benevolent smile lit up the room. "Good!" he said. "You got up during Brahma Muhurtham."

"Chidanandji!" Vivek cried. "How did you get in?"

"Not with a key," Chidanandji said matter-of-factly. "But first things first, I need a cup of coffee." Chidanandji motioned for Vivek to sit on the sofa while he got up and made his way into the kitchenette to make a pot of coffee. Instead of exercising his miraculous culinary powers to materialize a cup of java, he simply used the hotel's coffee pot, Starbucks coffee packet, creamer, and sugar.

Vivek called out from the next room, "Chidanandji, you said Brahma something-or-other when you saw me. I'm curious, what is Brahma?"

"I said Brahma Muhurtham[9]," Chidanandji answered as he carefully measured the water and poured it into the coffee pot. "That is Brahma's hour. When you get up early in the morning, between 3:00 a.m. and 6:00 a.m., you are vulnerable. The reason is that your false sense of protective armor, made up of thoughts, habits, and belief systems, is not yet fully functional. You are sort of suspended in your native state, where your deepest desires and anxieties are at the forefront of your consciousness, which makes you vulnerable, but also makes this the best time to minimize them or get rid of them altogether. This is the best time of the day to pray for that very reason." He placed the coffee pouch in the coffee pot, closed the lid and turned on the pot to brew the coffee. "Anyway, how are you, Vivek?"

"I wish I could say 'better,' Chidanandji," Vivek replied. "The peace I experienced with you that day in the cave lasted for only a few months. I'm desperately thirsting for that peace again. I'm not sure how you found me, but it's sure good to see you again. I feel like this is all a dream or something."

Chidanandji poked his head around the corner and grinned at Vivek, "No, you are not dreaming. But I have to say that I am a bit disappointed you did not take the positive energy you received from me and surge forward. Instead, you lived in the past and made your life more miserable. What's up with that?"

Vivek struggled to find an answer. "Well, I do not know any other way to live. While it's great to live in the present moment and being aware of life around you and within you, reality still comes knocking on your door like

---

[9]   Brahma Muhurtham: The early-morning hours between 3:00 and 6:00 a.m. This time is considered auspicious for contemplation. The Sanskrit word "Brahmam" refers to Supreme Consciousness also, just like "Atma."

an unwanted guest that tends to overstay his welcome. Instinctively, we follow our gut and sometimes end up in the gutter."

Chidanandji chuckled, seemingly at the thought of the folly and fate of humans. "Son, do not be too hard on yourself, I have not given up on you, as evidenced by the fact that I am here, just as I had promised you."

Vivek persisted. "Chidanandji, awareness is not that easy to master and maintain. Most people can't do it because their mind gets in the way. The never-ending stream of thoughts becomes the obstacle to peace."

Chidanandji walked back into the living room with two steaming cups of coffee. Offering Vivek a cup, he sat down and gingerly sipped from the mug. After savoring his first sip of morning coffee, he let out a contented sigh like an addict relieving the stress of an addiction, leaned back into the sofa, and turned his attention back to Vivek. "There's nothing like a good strong cup of coffee in the morning to waken one's senses." Vivek laughed at the sudden detour of conversation and at Chidanandji's enjoyment of the present moment and his freshly brewed cup of coffee. After delighting in his second sip of coffee, Chidanandji continued. "Good observation. But remember, patience is the key. You should never give up. As soon as you perceive falseness or pretense in yourself, you should change gears and go back to your original goal of becoming aware of awareness itself and nothing else."

Vivek's voiced echoed hollow in his ears. "Without you helping me achieve awareness, I drift back into my habitual state of thinking, desiring and worrying."

"It is but natural," consoled Chidanandji. "How can you suddenly change the habit developed over several births and assiduously practiced for thirty-six years in this birth? I understand."

"Am I the only one who struggles with this?" Vivek asked.

Chidanandji looked directly into Vivek's eyes before answering. "Son, everyone struggles with the concept of spirituality. Whole civilizations throughout history have struggled with this issue, as evidenced by the multitude of wars waged in the name of God, Jesus, Allah, and so on. Even

Jesus wasn't immune to questioning God's plan toward the end of his life. All great souls have faltered in their belief at some time or another, and have had their faith tested in their darkest hours. Like I say, every saint has a past and every sinner a future. Take me, for instance. I didn't become what I am overnight. It was an intense struggle. And although realization can happen in an instant, it's still a long and arduous life-long journey to get there. I struggled and struggled until one day God's grace dawned on me."

Vivek was puzzled. "So I have to believe in God for this to happen?"

Chidanandji replied, "You do not have to believe in anything. You just have to be yourself."

Vivek's confusion grew. "But I am myself," he persisted.

Chidanandji shook his head. "No, no. Not this limited self. You have to transcend the body, breath, mind, intellect and the heart through awareness."

"Yeah, but that's what I'm having problems with because I'm still tethered to my physical body and its immediate needs."

"If you're still so tethered to your body and needs, then how would you have been able to walk away from making all of the money you were making at your last job just to set up a trust fund worth millions of dollars?" Chidanandji questioned.

"What? How do you know about the trust fund?" Vivek asked.

Chidanandji looked down with a guilty look on his face. "Because it was I who inspired you from within to form it."

Vivek shook his head. "Wait a minute. How did you do that? Was it you that woke me up in the middle of the night with a voice in my head telling me to form the trust fund and help others? That was you?"

Chidanandji took another sip of his cooling coffee and replied, "No, that was your own inner voice. I just encouraged it and nurtured it. So how is it going?"

Vivek gulped the last of his coffee. "My friend Greg is helping me. We are reviewing several proposals and will soon decide which one to fund. The toughest challenge is not giving money, but to give it to the right organization with the right leadership so that they do not fritter the money away but use it to the fullest extent to help the needy. I do not want to encourage charlatans to cheat us and the needy people simultaneously," he answered.

Chidanandji agreed. "Yes, unfortunately, there are many vultures out there disguised as pigeons that are waiting to cheat you. You need to do extensive background checks and institute checks and balances to ensure that no such misuse happens or even if it does happen, that you can pull out right away."

Vivek set his mug down on the coffee table and took a deep breath before diving into the next question. "Chidanandji, even though I seem to have the power of free will to do anything, something else seems to control me and make me do things. So do I have free will or am I just a puppet of a destiny that affects every decision I make?"

Chidanandji laughed and stroked his beard. "Ahh, the mystery of man: Do you have free will or are you bound by the chains of destiny? Let me ask you this first, what do you think of Mendel, the Austrian priest and father of genetics[10]?"

Vivek's brain scanned the closed files of his high school and college education for the answer. "If I remember correctly he is famous for his laws of inheritance."

"Can you tell me briefly what his laws of inheritance are?"

"I don't remember exactly," said Vivek. "But the gist is this; children inherit genes from their parents. Certain traits which may not show in an individual can be passed on to the next generation."

---

[10]   Gregor Mendel was an Augustinian priest and scientist, and is often called the father of genetics for his study of the inheritance of certain traits in pea plants. Mendel showed that the inheritance of these traits follows particular laws, which were later named after him.

Chidanandji pressed. "That's right, and what about Watson and Crick?"

Vivek knit his brows together as he rummaged through his memory bank containing a lifetime of data. His eyes lit up as soon as he was able to extract the answer from one of the multitude of files residing in his mind. "They discovered DNA—deoxy ribonucleic acid. Okay, Chidanandji, as a guy who lives in a cave in a mountain, how do you know about Gregor Mendel and Watson and Crick?"

Chidanandji finished off his coffee and nodded. "The cosmic wisdom of the universe teaches me a great deal. Anyway, DNA is the code of life. It determines your skin color, eye color, height, what diseases you are prone to, etcetera. So genetics seem to prove that everything is predestined, from a scientific standpoint. But does that mean that just because your father is diabetic that you automatically will be, too? That's where free will steps in, Vivek." Chidanandji leaned forward and spoke with authority. "Suppose you follow a good organic, vegetarian diet, exercise regularly, sleep well, and exude a positive attitude about life? You can beat the odds and lead a healthy life. Common sense would dictate that this is evidence of free will."

Vivek shrugged. "I get it, but which among the two, destiny and free will, is the one that rules the other? They can't both be flip sides of the same coin."

"Aha, that's where you are wrong, son. They are indeed both dependent while at the same time, cannot exist without the other. Look at night and day, or the heat of summer offsetting the coldness of winter—these are examples of duality in nature and the universe. Opposites coexist, but only in the physical realm."

More confused than ever, Vivek said, "Please explain."

Chidanandji pointed to a glass of water. "Vivek, is this glass of water half empty or half full?"

Vivek shrugged again. "That depends on the observer's perspective. An optimist sees it as half full while the pessimist sees it as half empty."

Chidanandji waved his hand and the glass fell to the ground and broke, splashing the water all over the wooden floor. Vivek jumped to clean the floor while Chidanandji motioned him to stay seated.

"We will clean it up later," said Chidanandji. "I broke it on purpose. Now, tell me. Is the glass half empty or half full?"

Vivek exclaimed. "Are you kidding, Chidanandji? You just broke the glass and spilled the water everywhere. There is no glass!"

"Bingo! As long as there is a body there is destiny and free will—a glass half full and half empty. So if you make decisions based on the past, you are fulfilling your destiny. If you make them motivated by the future, then you override destiny with free will. If when you are living in the present moment, there is no ego to attach itself to the victimization of the past or the outcome of the future. Therefore, there is no destiny or free will in the present moment. You become liberated from the constant struggle of balancing the two powers of destiny and free will.

"Let me put it another way. Free will and destiny are related to the ego and have no power over the higher consciousness—what you call Divine Will. Many people mistake destiny as Divine Will, but that is incorrect.

"The experience of awareness is very well summarized by William Blake in his poem 'Auguries of Innocence':

> "To see a world in a grain of sand,
> And a heaven in a wild flower,
> Hold infinity in the palm of your hand,
> And eternity in an hour."

Chidanandji continued, "If we can step aside from our limitations and ambitions, and learn to simply observe our actions, something miraculous happens. A higher power—whatever it is—takes over, and everything fits into place. The sports players talk about being in the zone. You are unstoppable, unreachable, and incredible at that moment. The reason is, the motivating force is not the ego, but something that transcends the ego.

"So, the more aware you are, the less attached you will be. The more aware you are the more peaceful and blissful you will be, and the closer to God you will be."

Vivek started feeling vibrations and tingling sensations throughout his body. As he became more aware of his body, the vibration energy extended to his extremities.

He felt a heat in the base of his spine and all up along its length. He also felt pressure there, as well as some numbing pain. His sense of awareness became very acute. With his eyes closed, he could literally see through the dark, first through the epidermal layer of the eyelids and the region inside the cornea. He could sense strange appearances and a host of different colors.

Suddenly he was in a realm of bliss. He did not even have to make an effort to become aware or meditate. It was as if he were in autopilot mode.

He felt as if his body were very light, but his senses were very alert. He could hear distant sounds, as well as the underlying Om[11] vibrations, happening simultaneously at different frequencies. Even when Chidanandji stopped guiding him, it took him quite a while—ten or fifteen minutes—to come back to his normal consciousness. It was difficult for him to transition from that peace. Even the effort to open his eyelids seemed too painful and too gross.

He transitioned into a wakeful stage about a half hour later, when the hot rays of the sun hit him directly on the face. The whole room was filled with a faint smell of jasmine and rose. Chidanandji was not on his seat. Vivek presumed that he must have left while he was in deep meditation.

---

[11]   Om: The symbol of cosmic vibrations, representing the fundamental frequency of creation. Even cosmology talks about a background humming noise of the universe, which may also refer to the Om sound. "Om" is a Sanskrit word which is also pronounced as "aum," "a" representing the wakeful stage, "u" representing the dream stage, and "m" representing the deep sleep stage, with the silence that follows representing a fourth stage which is beyond human comprehension.

Vivek remembered the broken glass and got up to clean it, but to his amazement, it had miraculously reassembled itself and was sitting on the end table in the morning sun.

He could not believe what had happened. The only evidence that Chidanandji had come was the half-empty coffee pot and the cups on the end table.

Refreshed and rejuvenated, Vivek checked out of the hotel, and was soon on the road toward a new future he felt sure would be filled with promise and peace.

Chapter 5

Several months later, Vivek was busy with work and with his foundation. He had practiced his awareness sessions and had been fairly successful on one level, but was still frustrated that he could never feel the peace and bliss that he had experienced during his encounters with Chidanandji. He felt guilty that he was not living up to Chidanandji's expectations. His mind yearned for satsang[12] and the memory of Chidanandji haunted him. Deep down he wished that he could just turn around and that Chidanandji would magically reappear.

His parents continued to pressure him about an arranged marriage, but he was able to deflect and outmaneuver their pleas and manipulation. Friends kept calling him about continued business opportunities he would have jumped at in the past, but now he had little interest in such offers. He worked hard on the foundation, always keeping in mind what Chidanandji had told him: "Always do your work, but don't let your work outdo you."

One day in the spring, Vivek's friend Vaidya called him at work and asked whether he was interested in attending a gathering to hear a New Age speaker talk about spirituality. The sponsor of the event was one of the

---

[12] Satsang: Refers to a group activity in which spiritual wisdom is shared between spiritual aspirants or between a teacher and his pupils. Bible study or a church sermon are typical examples. The true meaning of satsang, however, is "sat" (truth) and "sang" (companionship), namely, companionship with truth or with one's own real essence.

richest Indians in New York City, who was graciously opening the doors of his majestic home to host the event.

Vivek glanced absentmindedly at his list of tasks and immediately became distracted. The last thing he wanted to do was go to a New Age lecture, which would only pale in comparison to his experiences with Chidanandji. Besides, he had a laundry list of things to do before the night was over. Just as he was about to say "no, thanks," he paused for a moment, switched gears, and instead said politely, "Vaidya, I'd love to go, but I'm really busy right now. Why don't you give me your cell number? If I can make it tonight, I'll call you." Vivek scribbled Vaidya's number on a piece of paper, though he had no intention of attending the event. As soon as he put the phone down, he crushed the piece of paper into a ball and tossed it into the wastepaper basket and turned his attention back to what he had been doing when the phone rang.

Twilight gently settled into the evening sky, the lights of the city glowing and winking. Vivek looked up from his work at the clock on his wall, rubbed the residue of research and meeting notes from his eyes, stretched his taut muscles to get the blood flowing again, and got up from his chair to start putting his day's work to rest. After organizing his notes and files in preparation for tomorrow's workday, he locked his office and headed over to the elevator, then rode down and strode out of the building. When he hit the street, the pleasant, slightly cool evening air refreshed him and woke him up. He suddenly remembered Vaidya's phone call and a thought flashed through his mind: What if this speaking engagement were a sign from Chidanandji? He spun around on his heel and quickly ducked back into the revolving door of his office building and back into the elevator. He hit the button as the door closed, then made straight for his office and the crumpled paper ball lying at the bottom of his wastepaper basket. When he'd retrieved it, he uncrumpled it and called his friend.

Vaidya agreed to pick him up from the office in a cab in twenty minutes. A half hour later, Vaidya and Vivek pulled up in front of a palatial neo-Italian house in the East 70s and noticed several people streaming into the entrance, only to be greeted by the hosts and ushered inside. As the two of them stepped out of the taxi and up to the door, the host, whose home it was, greeted them and introduced them to his wife, who then escorted them from the vast marble-floored foyer into a grand ballroom, where the event was taking place. As Vivek and Vaidya walked in, they joined a large gathering of people of all ages, races, and religions and both genders. Excited whispering rippled around the room and the energy of the gathered throng gained momentum, like a spark growing into a flame. The crowd resembled a tapestry of beliefs, woven together in their shared curiosity and spiritual hunger. Most of the audience members sat on the floor, while others took their positions on overstuffed chairs lining the walls. Servers milled around offering tea and pastries to fill the hunger of the stomach while the guests yearned to satisfy the hunger of the mind and soul.

Vivek and Vaidya settled on the floor with their thoughts and awaited the evening's guest speaker. "This person must be highly thought of if he was invited to speak at the home of one of the richest Indians in New York," Vivek mused as he gazed around the room at the expectant faces.

Presently a hush came over the room as the honored speaker arrived. Expecting to see an older gentleman of Indian descent, Vivek was shocked. A young Caucasian woman in her thirties, impeccably dressed in an Indian sari with a matching blouse entered the room and stood before the audience, a radiant smile of peace and hope lighting up her face. Vaidya whispered into Vivek's ear, "That is Amanda Singh, a family friend of the hosts. She's going to talk about Advaitha."

Vivek blurted out, "Amanda Singh?"

Vaidya whispered, "Yes, her father is Indian and her mother is English. Amanda did her PhD in Indian philosophy at Oxford."

Vivek was taken aback. The rational part of his mind insisted that Amanda Singh was too young to know anything about one of the most abstract and difficult to comprehend philosophies known to man. In addition, she was a seemingly friendly and outgoing woman, while the majority of the spiritual masters who taught about Advaitha were reclusive men.

Vivek had to admit that he was curious to hear what she had to say, as clearly were the majority of the attendees. She made her way gracefully around the room, greeting people as if she were on a first-name basis with all of them. When she approached Vivek, she gave him a heartfelt smile. She immediately noticed that his teacup was empty and asked a passing server if she could take the teapot. The server nodded, puzzled as to what the young woman and honored speaker had in mind and what her next step was going to be. Amanda turned back to Vivek with the teapot in hand and asked if he wanted some tea. Vivek nonchalantly shrugged, said "Sure," and held out his cup. She started pouring the hot liquid into his porcelain teacup as she introduced herself.

"How are you?" she said. "I'm Amanda." As she poured the tea with one hand, she carefully kept the tray below Vivek's cup to catch any overflow. Vivek tried to pull his cup away when it was full, but strangely, she kept on pouring until it was overflowing onto the tray. Amanda kept on pouring until the tray was almost full and about to overflow onto the carpet.

Amanda stopped and looked deep into Vivek's eyes. "Yes, I know. The tea is about to overflow onto the carpet. Look at the cup and you are looking into a mirror image of yourself. You are the cup. How can I convey any new insight when you are already filled with so many concepts and ideas that you hold dear?" She smiled and gracefully moved on to talk to other guests. Vivek was in a state of shock and also embarrassed that he had been caught questioning the depth of her knowledge. "How in the world did she read my mind?" he thought. "Wow! She is really intriguing!" Vivek resolved that he would try to keep an open mind and listen to Amanda, whatever she had to say.

The audience had also picked up on Amanda's first lesson of the evening. The room quieted down and the whispers trailed off, all attention settling on this young and outgoing spiritual teacher. She handed the teapot to a waiter, who whisked it away as Amanda proceeded to walk to the front of the room. As she began her lecture, she spoke authoritatively, yet with deep humility. Vivek's eyes focused on her like laser beams and his hearing sharpened to capture her every word and nuance.

Amanda looked around the room. "My humble salutations to my beloved spiritual mentor and to all of you assembled here. All of you embody the Divine, so watch your tendency to judge a book by its cover. I noticed that when I walked in, many of you had serious doubts about me." She glanced at Vivek. "I know what you are saying to yourselves: 'How could a young woman of mixed heritage know anything about Advaitha, which is reserved for the highest levels of human intelligence, austerity, and perseverance?' I totally understand your skepticism. In fact, my understanding of Advaitha, or of anything of this world or the other is very limited. But I am not so much concerned about my intelligence or my ability as I am about inspiring you. Informing is one thing and inspiring you to action is another. I will speak as Gurudeva ordains me. If my thoughts inspire, your glory is to him."

Vivek was impressed. Not only was she sincere, but courageous, too. He felt a tinge of guilt for having judged her too quickly.

Amanda continued on. "God and religion are not for the privileged few," she said. "Those who put forth such an idea are nothing but charlatans and cheats. How could the Supreme Consciousness not love everyone? However, let me go one step further and say that God *does* love everyone equally."

At this statement, the audience responded with enthusiasm. The room reverberated with the sound of clapping. But their joy did not last long because Amanda's next statement stunned them into silence.

"Yes, God *loves* each of us equally but cannot *treat* each of us equally."

The silence was deafening as the crowd tried to comprehend the dichotomy of Amanda's words. Vivek's interest peaked. "That is very intriguing!" he thought. "She is not only intelligent, but she's feeling the pulse of the audience."

One elderly gentleman raised his hand, "Daughter, you are not making sense. How can God love us equally but not treat us equally?"

A young man interjected, "How do you know what God does or does not do? If that's the case, then I do not want to believe in an unjust God."

Sensing the growing uneasiness, Vivek got up and said, "Ladies and gentlemen. Let us hear what our honored guest has to say. Let us not jump to conclusions. Can't we please suspend our judgment and listen to what she has to say? Did we not attend tonight to hear something that will change our lives for the better, to enlighten our journey of life here on earth? We can form our own opinions after we have more information to base them on, but for now please give her the freedom to express hers." The audience quieted down and soon there was a hush of silence again. The host glanced thankfully at Vivek while Amanda remained calm and unperturbed. She smiled appreciatively at Vivek as if he were an older brother out to protect her from harm.

Amanda continued. "I notice that my comments have caused a polarized set of emotions—joy, shock, trust, disbelief. We live in the world of dvaitha—of extremes: dark and light, pain and pleasure, heat and cold. It seems that duality is the essence of our existence, and that without one, you can't have the other.

"If you stand in front of the mirror, for example," Amanda continued, "Your image reflects back to you. A mirror image treats everyone equally and is impervious to the beauty of the person in the image. It just reflects. If the person is beautiful, the image will be beautiful. If the person is clean, the image will be clean. If the person is cruel, the image will look cruel. Ultimately, beauty is in the eye of the beholder.

"God, on the other hand, is more than a mirror. God reflects what is *within* us, while the mirror only reflects what is on the *outside*. If we are kind, God reflects kindness back to us. If we love others, we receive love from God. If we are selfish or downright cruel, God either ignores us or admonishes us. But through it all, God is the all-encompassing eternal witness. Love is the strongest and purest emotion that He responds to. Advaitha is love in feeling, thought, word, and deed. It is love in action, not a philosophy to be used as rhetoric for theoretical and academic discussions.

"According to yoga, there are four paths to perfection: through selfless action, through fine-tuning the body and the mind, through purifying the emotions, and through refining the intellect and intuition. These paths are intertwined and you can't have one without the other. For example, if you do not have good feelings, your action or karma will be useless. If you do not have a calm mind, your feelings will be turbulent and even destructive. If you do not understand the meaning of something, your mind will not be at peace. Ultimately all paths are based on the foundation of Advaitha, whether we acknowledge it or not."

As Amanda looked around and called for questions, a woman timidly raised her hand. Amanda smiled warmly at her and nodded in encouragement. The woman's voice quivered slightly with self-consciousness. "What is practical Advaitha? If you need to explain practical Advaitha, does it mean Advaitha in its purity is impractical?"

Suddenly the crowd was smelling blood. They were curious as to how Amanda was going to keep cool under fire and answer everyone's questions. Like a feeding frenzy, hands suddenly shot up all around the room. Unaffected by the sharks starting to swim around her, Amanda looked serenely around the room and encouraged them to ask more questions. In the next second, a stream of questions came at her from all directions.

"Will practicing Advaitha affect my lifestyle? Do I have to give up my home and visiting my grandchildren?"

"Does marriage come in the way of practicing Advaitha?"

"What about work? Is Advaitha opposed to work? Can a shrewd businessman be an Advaithin?"

"I want to join a Christian missionary and become a nun. Can I be a Christian nun and an Advaithin?" Heads craned around to locate the young American woman who had asked the question, but then, as if tracking a Ping-Pong game, the heads instantly swung in the opposite direction as a joker in the crowd bellowed out, "I like to crack jokes and make people laugh. Is Advaitha opposed to humor? Is Advaitha only for serious people with a constipated attitude?"

Vivek began to get irritated by the mockery of the group and didn't appreciate their callous attitude toward Advaitha and Amanda, whom he had begun to respect and admire. He stood up, faced the crowd and said, "I think the questions are a bit overboard and it seems like Ms. Amanda Singh is being attacked with a barrage of questions. I think that we would all agree that that's not being fair to her."

Amanda stepped forward and raised her hand to intervene. "Thank you, but I'm perfectly okay with the questions. Questions are good because the ensuing answers clarify matters, open the mind to new perspectives and knowledge, and change the way we think and act. There's nothing wrong with questions. In fact, there are no wrong questions, only wrong answers on occasion. Let me answer your questions in the order that they were asked."

"What is practical Advaitha? If you need to explain practical Advaitha, does it mean Advaitha in its purity is impractical? If Advaitha means there is no other, then what role does God play? Does Advaitha need or stand on the premise of a personal or impersonal God? And if you don't believe there is a God, then how do you explain order in the universe amidst the chaos? Do you have to change your lifestyle to practice Advaitha? Do you have to give up your home and visiting your grandchildren? Does marriage come in the way of practicing Advaitha? What about work? Is Advaitha opposed to work? Can a shrewd businessman be an Advaithin?"

She paused as if ruminating on her next statement. "And what about an Advaithin nun? Is there such a thing? Or even a nun who likes to laugh and tell jokes, for that matter? Or is Advaitha only for serious people with constipated attitudes?" Laughter erupted from the crowd as the feeding frenzy abated and curiosity took its place.

"Now for the answers. But first of all, let me assure you that Advaitha is not opposed to anything and can and does coexist with everything. This one statement answers almost all of your questions, as you will see.

"Advaitha is neither opposed to the concept of a personal or impersonal God, nor does it deny it or discredit it. Advaitha is a state of consciousness—supreme consciousness. Consciousness pervades everything and Advaitha is the noblest and purest aspect of consciousness. Advaitha is the only practical thing in our lives. Everything else we are doing, including the way we live our lives, is impractical. For example, it is easy to tell the truth and hard to tell a lie because you have to manage circumstances to protect that lie. Our life is a journey of pain, since we are trying to live the lie that we are just a body and not a soul. You may be shocked to hear that I called the body a lie. Let me explain. You are aware of your body during your wakeful stage when you are not distracted by your thoughts. During your dream stage and during deep sleep, you are not at all aware of your physical body. That which appears and then disappears during the day like a mirage cannot be the real truth and hence has to be a lie or at best our imagination.

"Being aware of Atma[13], your supreme consciousness, is like being in the eye of a hurricane. It is where peace prevails in the sea of life's chaos and confusion.

"You do not have to rearrange your life or ignore your grandchildren to be an Advaithin. An Advaithin loves her grandchildren and everyone else's grandchildren, too.

"Yes, you can marry or become a Christian nun or even be a stand-up comic and still be an Advaithin. Being an Advaithin has nothing to do with your physical appearance, your vocation, or your status in life. It's like asking if space is opposed to physical and mental characteristics. Humans, animals, and even worms live in this physical space, which we call the cosmos, irrespective of their characteristics, lifestyles, and aptitudes. We all exist in space, but the space has nothing to do with us. Instead of space, we exist in the consciousness of our inner spirit.

"Human minds and lives are entrenched in duality. We like warmth; we dislike cold. We like pleasure; we dislike pain. We like appreciation; we dislike criticism. We like fun; we dislike responsibility. In everything we do, we want to maximize one over the other. We want to do only acts that give us maximum joy and minimal pain. We want to maximize our pay, but minimize our workload. But no matter what we do, we fail to gain undiminished bliss and undisturbed peace. In spite of our best attempts to be happy, we end up being unhappy. In spite of our best attempts to be popular, we end being unpopular. In spite of our best attempts to control everyone around us, we end up being totally out of control ourselves. Why?"

Amanda took note of the puzzled faces sprinkled throughout the room. "Let me explain. In 1975, a gentleman named Barry Johnson came up with a new concept. At one time, he was a motivational speaker speaking to large audiences of CEOs and decision-makers from some of the largest Fortune 500 companies. They had all come to his workshops to learn how

---

[13]   Atma: Refers to the universal indwelling spirit which permeates all of creation, just as space permeates all of the physical cosmos. "Atma" is another name for supreme consciousness.

to build teams, how to motivate workers, how to increase productivity and reduce cost, and how to enhance customer confidence.

"Barry surprised everyone by saying, 'You have all been attending my team-building conferences every year, yet how many of you have truly achieved your goals? The reality is, you have only marginally succeeded. Think about it: If you had really succeeded, you wouldn't be here today. There would be no need for you to come back. So obviously what you are doing is not working.'

"Shock began to register around the room, and then disbelief turned into anger. How could this famous motivational speaker with the stellar reputation for arming executives to build their empires and run global conglomerates discredit his own knowledge and expertise? How could he have taken their millions of dollars to conduct these workshops and then turn around and claim that they didn't work? And to rub salt in the wound, he was also calling them fools and telling them that they were wasting their time, resources, and energy!

"What Barry Johnson then went on to discuss that day has changed the way management looks at solving difficult or impossible problems. He talked about being bold and innovative with new changes while at the same time being conservative to preserve the value of the company. He also encouraged teamwork and cooperation, as well as individual growth and development. His approach to duality even extended to reducing production costs without sacrificing manufacturing quality, or home commitments versus work commitments. The list goes on and on.

"The point is, you can't solve problems by choosing one over the other. The nature of the duality is that each is one side of the same coin. You can't have one without the other. Unfortunately, we tend to choose one over the other and live in denial, not facing the consequences of our decisions and actions. These challenges are what we call polarities (or dilemmas, or paradoxes), which are inherently unavoidable and unsolvable. The ongoing natural tension between the poles can be destructive and debilitating and hence has to be *managed* and channeled into a creative synergistic force that leads to superior outcomes.

"You cannot maximize one and minimize the other. You need to manage both. Similarly, the problem of how to lead a peaceful life in the world and gain spiritual wisdom is also a polarity. The middle path[14] suggested by the Buddha or the teachings of the Bhagavad Gita are solutions for how to manage these polarities. Advaitha is the basis on which the solution to polarities rests. However, the root cause of the problem of polarities is the human ego.

"People ask, 'What is ego?' When you get a prompting to do something like drink coffee or eat sweets, or even if you start to feel like murdering somebody, ask yourself, 'Who is really bossing me? Who is behind the scenes and running the show? When did I give him or her the authority to tell me what to do?' That is the ego, which is rooted in the human mind. And the human mind will do whatever it can to survive, to be accepted and liked and noticed by others, even if it operates out of greed, anger, stress, and frustration—the elements all linked to fear.

Heads started nodding around the room as the concept began to sink in. Amanda continued, "Basically, there are four types of people. First of all, there are people who respond to every thought. These folks live by their instincts and are, for the most part, closed-minded and ignorant. Second, there are people who only respond to information that benefits them, or brings them instant gratification. Then there is the third group of folks, who respond to information only if it is for the good of all. And finally, there are those enlightened souls who do not respond to any thought or piece of information, but impartially observe it as if observers of the drama of their life.

"Our ego is like the chain of gravity that holds us down. Our ego emanates from our brain, which is designed to fear and survive rather than learn and grow. It's the mechanism that safeguards our physical body, but it is not the gatekeeper of our souls. Our souls are founded on love and peace, while our brains feed on fear and familiarity. What is not familiar to us creates fear in our minds because the unpredictability of the future triggers our

---

[14]   The Middle Path: Refers to not taking recourse in extremes. For example, both fasting and feasting will destroy a person's health; however, moderate consumption of food will result in healthy living. Too much sleep or too much activity will cause mental imbalance; however, moderate sleep tempered by moderate activity will foster a healthy and peaceful mind.

survival instincts. That's where the duality exists—in the mind. Therefore, our brain and ego become our bondage. We need to detach ourselves from bad and good and eventually from all of our thoughts, good or bad. Behind every thought there is the root thought, the 'I' thought, which is neither good nor bad. Awareness is being immersed in this 'I' thought. This is also known as the 'I' principle."

There was a slight shuffling in the room as the attendees leaned forward in anticipation of Amanda's next statement. "You cannot solve the problem," she said, "while being in the same domain where the problem originated. You have to detach mentally and step outside of your life to fully observe it in order to rise above the problem to seek the solution that is already within your reach. And guess what?" Amanda paused, savoring the anticipation of the crowd. She knew that she held them in the palm of her hand and she knew to hold them gently. "Detachment is natural to all of us. When we go to sleep, for example, we detach from our wakeful state. When we fall into deep sleep, we detach from our dream state. When we wake up, we detach from our deep sleep.

"We have approximately sixty-five thousand thoughts per day. And ninety-five percent of those thoughts are repeated the next day. And now we're bombarded with so much more information living in our increasingly connected world. However, the space between our thoughts is the most important because that's where we are totally free and peaceful. The silence between our thoughts is where our consciousness resides and the true source of joy because our mind is totally at rest.

"Modern science and psychology teach us that the objective world is real and the subjective—or inner—world is all imagination. But the truth is the exact opposite: The objective world is unreal and the subjective, or inner, world is relatively unreal, too, however, it is a lot closer to reality. Therefore, the ignorant man who identifies himself with his body and mind is dying every moment, along with every perception or thought. Yet when we identify ourselves with the changeless 'I' principle, we live on and know no death.

"We talk about living in the power of now. 'NOW' as an acronym means 'Never One Worries.'

"Now, we all experience deep sleep every day, even though we're not aware of it and don't know what happens in the process. Yet we awake totally refreshed, peaceful, and energetic. Deep sleep is the key to understanding our reality. Understand what deep sleep is. You will understand everything you need to understand."

Murmurs broke out around the room and heads nodded enthusiastically in agreement. Amanda gestured with confidence and passion for her subject. "In comparison to other forms of knowledge, consciousness reigns supreme. Consciousness is the purest form of knowledge that already exists within us."

Amanda went on talking for another fifteen minutes before concluding. She stopped for a brief moment to bring the audience's attention sharply in focus to end the discussion.

"In summary," she said, "Our mind and thoughts, while holding vast pieces of information that could propel us forward in knowledge and truth, in actuality, hold us back from our true state of consciousness, love, and peace. We must put our brains aside to discover our true nature, to live in the present moment and to truly live our lives. Because the simplicity and beauty of the present moment is where you will find true happiness. Don't put your life on hold as your brain is constantly trying to piece together the future to make it more predictable and favorable to its survival. Live your life now. I wish you all peace, prosperity and happiness. And at this time, our hosts have graciously prepared a dinner in the garden that you are all invited to. I thank them for giving me this opportunity to share my thoughts, ideas, and experiences with you tonight." The room resounded with applause while Amanda mouthed "thank you" to the audience, bowing her head in gratitude.

The crowd began to get up, stretch their legs and move down the hall into the garden. Amanda waited patiently in the front of the room to shake hands and answer any further questions before politely making her way through the crowd. As she walked through the crowd she was again greeted with handshakes and kudos from enthusiastic participants. Before long, she appeared before Vivek, who was patiently waiting to talk with her while the crowd streamed past him, hungry for more than just enlightened information. Amanda extended her hand to him and to his surprise, he noticed a gold chain around her neck that held a picture in a locket: a picture of Chidanandji. He looked at her with shock and disbelief at the significance of the coincidence. He couldn't help but notice the mischievous look on her face. She leaned forward and whispered in his ear, "I did not come here to lecture. It was a ploy and excuse, planned by Chidanandji. The main reason I came here is to meet you. I have a message for you."

Chapter 6

Vivek's eyes widened. How could it be that Amanda had a message for him from Chidanandji?

Amanda smiled. "He told me all about you, and specifically asked me to come today here to meet you. He also said you may continue to call him Chidanandji, since you have not yet accepted him as your guru." She glanced around at the crowd milling past her as they streamed into the garden. The host and hostess had clearly outdone themselves, with candlelit linen-covered tables that held vases of cascading Monet-inspired flowers. The colors of the blossoms danced against the backdrop of the candlelight and reflected off the water glasses. Waiters carrying platters of food maneuvered carefully between the tables as the attendees streamed in. The conversations floating around the garden gained momentum as more attendees gathered there, creating a crescendo effect.

"It's crowded out here," Amanda observed. "We won't be able to talk to each other unless we yell across the table. Why don't we go somewhere else where we can hear each other talk?"

Vivek agreed and told her that he would be right back. He went to find Vaidya in the crowd to let him know he was leaving, and found him talking to a couple of older gentlemen.

As he approached, Vivek overheard one gentleman comment on the new health-care reform. Before he could go any further, Vivek interrupted what was sure to turn into a heated debate and told Vaidya he was leaving. When he explained why, surprise registered on Vaidya's face.

"Huh?" he said. "How could it be that she's here to give you a message from Chidanandji? Man, that dude must really be trying to reach you. It's weird that he's not doing it by email but through Amanda. Of course you have to talk to her and figure this whole thing out. Gee, it's almost like your life has turned into a mystery novel. I can't wait to hear how it ends. At any rate, don't worry about me, buddy. You just have to promise me you'll let me know how it goes."

"I will," said Vivek. "But first, I want to introduce you to Amanda before we head out."

He steered his friend through the throng of people to where Amanda was talking with the hosts. After Vivek had walked away, the hosts had approached her, thanking her for being the guest of honor and keynote speaker, and had apparently invited her to sit at the head of the table in the designated seat of honor.

"Oh, that's sweet of you," Amanda was saying. "Thank you for inviting me. Unfortunately, I have another commitment that I must attend to. I hope you understand and I do look forward to coming back and continuing our dialogue."

She looked over at Vivek and Vaidya, who had joined the group. Smiling, she introduced the pair. The hosts turned to the friends. Vivek and Vaidya shook their hands and thanked them for putting on the event, which had drawn so many people.

"Amanda's presentation was enlightening," the hosts agreed. "We have attended her discussions in the past and wanted to open our home so that others could hear her talk and learn how to live their lives differently and be happy and peaceful. We hope we are doing the same thing in our own way by opening our hearts and our home to others."

"Vaidya," the hostess said, "Why don't you sit with us at the head of the table since Amanda and Vivek are leaving? We would like to hear more about how you learned about the event." Vaidya was only too happy to accept their invitation. They said their goodbyes and headed toward the garden while Amanda located her coat and purse.

As they made their way out of the front door, Amanda rummaged through her purse and carefully pulled out a small envelope and handed it to Vivek. Vivek's heart quickened as he took the note and read it in the dim light of the front steps while Amanda looked for a cab.

The note, like his name on the envelope, was written in English on paper saturated with the scent of vibudhi[15] mixed with jasmine and rose—a signature smell of Chidanandji—and it read:

> Reflection of My Self:
>
> Accept my blessings! Amanda, who brings this note, is a long-time friend and acquaintance. Do come to Gangotri[16] on the Vaishak Poornima[17] day. I will be waiting for you on the banks of Ganga.[18] Amanda is a very mature soul. Learn as much from her as you can.
>
> With love and more blessings,
> Chidanand
>
> Note: By the way, keep the teacup always empty!

Vivek felt a small shiver ripple up his spine. Chidanandji had asked him to come to the source of the Ganges River in the Gangotri glacier. He didn't have a clue as to when Vaishak Poornima was supposed to occur. He turned to Amanda. "When did Chidanandji give you this message?"

"Two weeks ago at Rishikesh, just before I left," she replied.

---

[15]   Vibudhi: Sacred ash to be worn on the forehead or smeared over the body as a symbol of renunciation, as well as a symbol of the unreality of the phenomenal universe. Since ash cannot be further transformed into something else, it is supposed to represent the ultimate immutable and unchangeable reality.

[16]   Gangotri: The glacier which is the source of the river Ganges. "Gangotri" literally means "where the Ganges originates."

[17]   Vaishak Poornima: The full moon day in the month of Vaishak in the Hindu lunar calendar.

[18]   Ganga: The River Ganges, which is worshipped as a goddess.

"What?" Vivek was puzzled. "He's not at Thiruvannamalai?"

Amanda looked intently into Vivek's eyes before replying. "Vivek, he can be wherever he wants to be. Why are you asking?"

Vivek handed her the note. "He wants me to be there on the Vaishak Poornima. When is that?"

"Today is the first day of month of Vaishak. Vaishak Poornima falls on the fourteenth day from today," Amanda said. She raised her eyes slowly up to Vivek's as she handed back the note. "I've heard that Chidanandji has a hermitage in Gangotri."

Upon hearing her words, Vivek's heart quickened in anticipation and trepidation. "It looks like I don't have a lot of time," he said. "I'll need to leave for India next week." Amanda nodded in agreement. Vivek felt tendrils of panic weave through his veins. "Amanda, I'll need some help because I don't know anything."

Amanda placed a reassuring hand on Vivek's arm and said, "I know. That's why he sent me."

As she uttered those words, the hairs on Vivek's arm stood on end. He shivered slightly, yet felt a warm feeling of comfort and peace come over him. Amanda smiled her knowing smile again and turned to wave down a cab as it rounded the corner and headed down the street toward them. Vivek held the door for her, then slipped in beside her in the back seat, still reverently holding Chidanandji's note as if it were a treasured ancient artifact. His stomach started to rumble. Hoping that Amanda hadn't noticed, he was about to say something about his upcoming trip, but was interrupted in his thoughts when Amanda said, "I know you're hungry. Let's go down to the West Village to one of my favorite restaurants and grab a bite to eat." Vivek, in the meantime, hoped that they reached the restaurant before his stomach started growling again.

Soon the taxi pulled up in front of a small restaurant nestled on a quiet, tree-lined street. Vivek went to pull out his wallet, but Amanda waved him away. She gave the driver a generous tip, then said to Vivek as they stepped out onto the curb, "This is a vegetarian restaurant. I think you'll like the food, and we'll at least be able to have a quiet conversation here."

Vivek glanced at his watch, which read 10:35 p.m. "Are they still open this late?"

Amanda nodded. "They close at 10:30, but don't worry," she reassured him. "The owners know me. Their daughter was a classmate of mine at Oxford."

Vivek wasn't feeling half as sure as Amanda, particularly when he saw the "CLOSED" sign hanging on the inside of the door's window and the last of the patrons inside finishing up their meals. Amanda didn't seem to notice and nonchalantly rang the bell.

As they waited patiently on the sidewalk, Vivek looked up and saw the sign for the restaurant. He looked away for a half a second and sharply snapped his attention back to the sign. The coincidence didn't escape his attention. The sign displayed a colorful teapot pouring tea into dainty porcelain cup, with the words "The Tea Cup" below.

Suddenly the door opened and an elderly gentleman appeared with a questioning look, but the look was soon replaced with a look of recognition. His eyes widened as he flashed a huge smile at Amanda.

"Uncle," she said, "this is Vivek, a favorite of Chidanandji's. Vivek, this is Uncle Farhat Towfiq, and Auntie Mirium Towfiq is over there." She motioned to the right of the entrance to where a woman was talking to a table of patrons finishing their desserts. "They're from Iran and follow the Baha'i faith and are devotees of Chidanandji."

Amanda continued, "I'm sorry I'm barging in this late, Uncle. How is Jwaleh?" Vivek wondered if Jwaleh was their daughter. "We are famished and were wondering if we could still get something to eat."

The owner held the door open to invite them in. "Of course, Amanda. You know you are welcome here any time of the day or night. I can heat up the vegetable stew you love and serve it with seven-grain toast."

Amanda smiled as she hugged him like a doting daughter. "Can I have some of my favorite saffron tea, too?"

"Of course, dear." Mr. Towfiq grabbed a couple of menus and led them to the back of the restaurant. He motioned to a small table set for two in a quiet corner, and once they were seated, he bustled off to get the stew, toast, and tea. Strains of exotic music played in the background, a woman's voice gliding effortlessly over the notes.

The aroma of saffron filled the room and grew stronger as a teapot was set before them. Amanda poured the tea into their cups and Vivek found himself falling into a bit of trance. The sultry sounds and smells of the restaurant created a hypnotic effect, almost lulling him into a different state of consciousness. A peaceful feeling came over him until his stomach alerted him again to the fact that it was demanding to be fed. He knew dinner was on the way, and attempted to distract himself by turning his thoughts to the note.

He sipped the tea and resumed his conversation with Amanda. "Why did Chidanandji ask me to come to Gangotri for Vaishak Poornima?" he asked.

Amanda set her teacup down. "Vaishak Poornima, the full moon, happens in April or May and is significant because it marks the day that Buddha was born. This is also the day that he reached Nirvana[19] and the day he chose for his Maha Samadhi[20]."

"Huh," Vivek said, "I didn't know that. Is there a reason that Chidanandji would pick that day?

Amanda began to reply but was cut short by Vivek's phone playing a rendition of Led Zeppelin's "Stairway to Heaven." She arched her eyebrows as Vivek rolled his eyes.

---

[19]   Nirvana: The state of final emancipation from suffering.

[20]   Maha Samadhi: Samadhi means the experience of total equanimity while alive. Generally, samadhi is short-lived and is experienced only for a few hours or days. However, Maha Samadhi means the experience of permanent and total equanimity that one experiences after death. A person who has attained Maha Samadhi is never born again.

"Yep, I'm a big fan. It's a long story. Do you mind if I take this call?"

"Not at all," Amanda replied. "I understand."

He glanced at the phone before answering. "Hey, Greg," he said.

Greg Keaton's booming voice transcended the iPhone's built-in speaker. "Hey, buddy, where in the heck are you? I need you to sign a couple of large checks for the foundation. I'm going to hand them over first thing tomorrow to the person in charge of the service organization that we approved. When can you come over to sign them?"

Vivek shifted in his seat. "Greg, I'm having dinner with someone right now." His eyes met Amanda's. "Why don't we meet first thing in the morning to take care of it?"

"Oh, sure, buddy. I didn't mean to interrupt anything." From his tone of voice, Vivek gathered that Greg's mind was conjuring up all sorts of ideas as to who Vivek was spending time with and what would follow dinner. "But you're not planning on running off somewhere again, are you, and leaving me in the lurch? Remember, you promised me that you would take me to India with you the next time you went."

Guilt washed over Vivek as if he had just been caught in a lie and he felt a pressing need to confess. "Greg, I am actually planning on taking off to India, but not in the way that you think. I just received a note from Chidanandji inviting me to come to India, so I can't bring you with me on this trip. The next one, I promise. I hope you understand. We can talk about it more in the morning. I'm going to need to travel to India within a week, but don't worry, I'll finish up as many things regarding the foundation as I can before I leave. How about meeting for breakfast at our usual place at eight?"

"You got it," said Greg, and told Vivek to be sure to have fun with his dinner date. Vivek chuckled and hung up. He turned back to Amanda, who sat patiently sipping her tea with an amused smile.

"So that was Greg Keaton?" she said.

"What? You know Greg Keaton? How could that be?"

"Because," Amanda explained, "Chidanandji told me about him and about your noble work at the Awareness Foundation."

Vivek looked at her intently. "Is there anything that you don't know about me?"

"Not really," she said mischievously.

Vivek laughed and shook his head in wonderment. "Well, in any case, I still have to figure out how to get to Gangotri."

Amanda leaned back as Mr. Towfiq reappeared with the stew and toast and carefully placed the food in front of them. She motioned for Vivek to fill his bowl with stew and continued her discussion. "You've been to Rishikesh, right?" Vivek nodded. "It's perhaps a day's journey from Rishikesh. I don't really know how to get there, but I would guess that you'd need to pass Badrinath[21], Kedarnath[22] and perhaps Yamunotri[23] along the way. I'd suggest landing in Rishikesh a couple of days before Vaishak Poornima and I'm sure Chidanandji will take over from there."

Vivek hoped that Amanda was right. He didn't relish the thought of being stranded in Rishikesh waiting for Chidanandji, who might not even show up. "Yeah, but it's really weird for me to plan a spur-of-the-moment trip," he said. "If you do indeed know me, then you know that I always follow a plan for everything. Serendipity is not my strong suit. I don't even know what to expect when I get there or how long I'll be there. I'm not comfortable doing things in a hurry like this and not knowing what to expect."

---

[21]   Badrinath: Sacred Himalayan temple dedicated to Lord Vishnu, the protector among the trinity of Gods.

[22]   Kedarnath: Sacred Himalayan temple dedicated to Lord Shiva, the destroyer among the trinity of Gods.

[23]   Yamunotri: The source of the river Yamuna.

Amanda laughed. "Well, then, now you can start to live. Living in the present moment and being happy is not about planning. When you plan everything, you replace simplicity with complexity. You also replace the happiness of discovering wonderful things by accident, which is what serendipity is, with fear of the unknown. You also replace your happy, loving self, which reflects your true nature, with an intense attitude focused on sticking to your plan. Serendipity is the art of living in the present moment. Tell your brain to step aside and let your soul breathe and your intuition guide you. That's where there is no fear. Just have fun and take the road less traveled."

Instinctively, Vivek knew she was right but his fear of the unknown still held sway over his thoughts. "Amanda, living from moment to moment is a scary thought to me. It goes against everything I have learned from school and about life. We're taught to be strategic in order to get ahead and succeed. Without a plan, you run the risk of failing. And I am a free spirit and an independent thinker." He continued, "And yet, while I think highly of Chidanandji, I also like my freedom and don't want to have him run my life. How long am I supposed to be there? Days, months?" Vivek shook his head and looked to Amanda for the answers. "In his note, Chidanandji mentioned that I should learn as much from you as I can. So how did you become so devoted to him? And how come he talks so highly of you? I'm curious."

Amanda finished up the last bite of her stew before responding. "Vivek, I understand your fear of the unknown. It's the same fear that made you afraid of the dark or of talking to strangers when you were little. If you didn't fear, then you wouldn't be human. The perception is that fear is what helps you survive in the physical world. That's what your brain is telling you. Love, on the other hand, casts aside the fear and puts you on a different trajectory. Believe me, Chidanandji is full of love—just as your true nature is, too.

"Don't be seduced by the honeycomb of thoughts that you're stuck in," she warned. "You say that you relish your freedom, yet you remain a slave to your thoughts. You can't be free if you live in fear from moment to moment. You run your life by preconceived notions, past experiences, habits, outdated beliefs, and reactive emotions and desires. True freedom is freedom *from* thinking, not freedom *of* thinking."

Vivek had to agree, since her point made perfect sense. "Yeah, but it's easier said than done. We're only human."

"Yes, but we are spirits, too, having a physical experience that you are referring to as being human." Amanda sipped the last of her tea. "Get over yourself, Vivek, and see yourself as so much greater than your mind and body. What? You think that energy only created your mind and body? Think again." She shifted in her seat and rested her arms on the table. "Your body is no different than the clothes you put on every day. The clothes don't do much hanging in a closet. But they transform when you wear them. The same goes for the body and the soul. The body is merely a vessel for your soul and becomes a way for it to experience the physical world and to learn from its experiences. Life is the ultimate school you'll ever experience. Your soul is observing life through your body. Chidanandji always says that the soul examines, experiences, evaluates, and enjoys life—the four E's."

Vivek responded, "But I do want to do the right thing and don't want to feel forced into doing it. I just want it to happen naturally."

Amanda peered intently into Vivek's eyes. "Vivek, the biggest problem with religions around the world, aside from the fact that they represent hierarchical structures of control and dominance, is that they preach that you have to use the ego to get rid of the ego. People fall into the trap of thinking that if they follow the rules, they will become spiritual. It doesn't even dawn on them that they already are spiritual and don't need gatekeepers to tell them how to get there. Your brain is always looking for ways to tell itself that it is special. It glorifies in its accomplishments and material possessions because it feels that these things define its existence. It falsely wants to feel superior to others and condemns and judges others as not being as spiritual, as knowledgeable, or as wealthy as it is. It seeks to compare and contrast because fear exists in differences."

She went on. "So many preachers extol the virtues of spirituality yet are only entertainers on stage for their own gratification. Or the professors who tout their intelligence yet fail to listen to the truths in others and learn more. There is no one more foolish than an educated fool. There is no one more dangerous than an entertaining evangelist. And look what's happening with the distorted views of any fanatic faith that believes that the path to God is found in the killings of innocent people. The blind cannot lead the blind except into greater ignorance, oblivion and perdition."

She leaned back in her chair. "Chidanandji likens the body to a corporation. The ego is the CEO, the mind the Chief Operating Officer, the intellect the Chief Technology Officer, the memory the Chief Financial Officer, the breath we take the Chief Information Officer, and the heart the Chief Relationship Officer. Our senses play a key role as project and program managers overseeing and disseminating all of the incoming information for the higher-level executives. The innumerable cells and organs in the body and the nerves are like employees. Traditionally everyone in the corporate environment dances to the tune of the CEO and the CFO. In some instances, the CTO and the CRO may challenge the CEO and more than likely they will be replaced. The COO always carries out the CEO's plan. Similarly, the mind obeys the ego and the senses follow suit, along with the prana[24] and the memory. On rare occasions, the intellect and the heart may question and challenge the ego, but they are quickly silenced like whistleblowers. The supreme consciousness, or God, is the chairman of the board and the body's consciousness, or the soul, is the investor. In rare moments of inspiration, the soul may break association with ego/mind complex and align itself with God, and that is when the inspiration happens."

"Hmm." Vivek drew in a breath and let it out slowly as he chewed on his thoughts. "I like the analogy. It resonates with the corporate-run society we live in. So the question is, how does our soul override this ingrained system?"

"Stay in the space between your thoughts," Amanda replied. "That's where the eternal peace is found. When you're constantly thinking, you're too distracted and limited by all the sensory data around you. There is no peace if you're always reading emails, watching TV, answering your phone, texting others or Googling all day long. Your brain is simply on steroids at that point."

---

[24]   Prana: Breath and vital air.

"It's hard to focus on the space between thoughts," Vivek said. "Every time I try to meditate, my perpetual lists of things to do keeps entering my mind."

"It takes practice," Amanda reminded him. "Everything happens at the right time. And speaking of time, it's getting late and you have to meet with Greg early in the morning and begin planning your trip. Let's say our goodbyes to Uncle and Auntie so that they can also go home halfway early. I'm going to catch another cab and head back uptown. If you'd like, I can drop you off at your place."

"But—" Vivek still had many questions to ask and was waiting for the ones he had already asked to be answered.

Amanda gently placed her hand on his arm. "Don't worry. Tell your brain to take a time-out and be reassured that all of your questions will be answered in time. You can't take in all of this information at once because it would be like trying to read all of the books in a library and trying to remember everything. It's impossible."

They got up and said their goodbyes to the Towfiqs and left the restaurant. On the ride back to Vivek's apartment, they fell silent so that Vivek could digest not only his food from dinner, but also Amanda's words of wisdom. The two of them sat quietly in the back seat, left to their thoughts as the lights of the city slipped past.

Chapter 7

Vivek pushed open the doors of his favorite breakfast spot and walked in. Smells of coffee greeted him, along with the sounds of dishes clinking, conversations, and frying bacon. He spotted Greg in a booth and joined him. The first thing he said was, "Don't ask about my dinner date. Nothing happened. She's just a good friend. Okay?"

Greg shrugged and grinned. "Okay, no questions asked."

The two went to work over breakfast and afterwards relaxed over coffee while Vivek told Greg about his upcoming trip. He promised Greg that he would contact him exactly one month after he left, no matter where he was, to let him know what was going on.

"Be careful and have a great time," Greg said.

Greg's words echoed in Vivek's mind long after they left the restaurant. He was grateful that his friend and business partner understood the significance of this journey and trusted him to run the foundation when he was gone.

Vivek called his parents to tell them that he would be traveling again. His mom was devastated, and seemed to think that she was going to lose her son forever. His father, on the other hand, simply muttered, "Son, I hope you know what you are doing. Don't come back and tell me that I did not warn you." Vivek understood their fears but felt sure that they would understand once he had the chance to explain it all to them when he got back.

He set out to shop for warm clothes. The bipolar Himalayan weather of extreme hot and cold required more than just T-shirts and jeans.

Afterwards, as he put his bags of new clothes in his car, he was suddenly seized with panic. "What the heck am I doing?" he thought to himself. "I don't even really know this Chidanandji. I don't know anything about him. He may have some kind of powers, but maybe it's not for good, but for something bad. And how come Amanda seems to know so much about me, yet I don't know anything about her? She never answered my questions about how she even met Chidanandji in the first place. Can I even trust her? Why am I being drawn into this?" He began to doubt his decision to meet Chidanandji again and didn't answer Amanda's call the next day.

Fear gripped him as he realized that it was next to impossible to run a background check on Chidanandji or Amanda before he left on his trip. And it didn't help matters any when he replayed Amanda's voice message. "Hi, Vivek how are you? I have been thinking about how fortunate you are that Chidanandji has invited you to come to Gangotri. That's an honor that has yet to be bestowed on me. I sincerely pray that you decide to go."

A couple more days passed by as the Vivek's silence grew into a resounding roar. He kept changing his mind every hour about the validity of his decision. He wanted to go, and yet did not want to go. He wished he could split his personality and send one to meet with Chidanandji and have the other stay in New York and work on his foundation. Several doses of aspirin still didn't reduce the headache that was growing by the minute.

Amanda left another message on Tuesday. This time she sounded more concerned. "Vivek, I have not heard from you. I know you are probably freaking out about this. Just let go of your fear and know that Chidanandji will guide you. You'll be fine, I promise. If you need me, please call any time of the day or night. I am here to help you."

Vivek felt the warmth in her voice and the affection in her heart. But he was not ready to call her back. By the time Vivek listened to her message, it was evening and he was on his way out of a meeting. He'd come a long way out of his way to attend the meeting, and it had been very stuffy and boring. He needed some breathing room and some time to think. Instead of taking a cab, as he usually did, he found himself boarding the subway for a long ride so that he could mull over his options. He sat down and noticed that there were a few tired New Yorkers anxious to get home after a long day at work. The doors closed and the train lurched forward and headed to its next destination.

Along the way, Vivek ruminated on his options and decided once and for all that he was going to stay in New York and not go to the Himalayas to meet Chidanandji. His angst of not knowing what he was going to do began to melt off of him in the heated subway and for once, he started to feel calmer. He also noticed that the remaining passengers had exited and that he was the only one left.

Suddenly the train came to a screeching halt. The doors opened and a stately gentleman in his early sixties entered wearing a hat and sunglasses. Vivek thought that it was strange that someone would wear sunglasses at night on a subway, but figured that the man was perhaps eccentric and shifted his attention away. The gentleman looked around at the rows of empty seats, and chose to stroll over and sit across from Vivek. "Great," Vivek thought. "It figures. He better not try anything stupid."

The gentleman spoke. "Do you mind if I sit here?" His accent sounded Scottish.

"No, go ahead. Be my guest," Vivek replied and noticed that he was clutching a brown envelope. Suspicion seeped into Vivek's mind and he prayed that the package was just that and not a weapon.

Vivek closed his eyes but then he got an eerie feeling that the gentleman was looking at him, so he decided to stay awake and on his guard.

The gentleman was indeed watching him. He smiled and spoke again. "You seem a bit tired. Long day, I presume?"

"Yes, you could say that."

"Pardon me for disturbing you," the gentleman said.

"It's fine," Vivek replied.

"Are you from New York?" asked the gentleman. "I can't help but notice that you are of Indian origin. Sometimes it's hard to tell anymore where folks are from, although it's a bit easier to figure out where I come from." He chuckled.

"I was born here. My parents came from India," Vivek said, wondering why this man was digging for information.

"Oh, India is indeed a beautiful country," the man remarked. "I've traveled there continually since I was a teenager. My favorite place to visit is the Himalayas. It's spectacular. You should go there when you're given the chance. Believe, me, you'll never forget the experience."

Vivek suddenly became alert. He sat up in his seat with a shocked expression on his face. "What, the Himalayas? You've been there?"

"Oh, yes, many times," the man murmured and glanced out the window as if in a dreamlike state. "I've actually camped there. I love to hike the mountains. It's so peaceful. I swear, there must be something in the water or air there. It's pure, wholesome and refreshing . . . or shall I say holy."

Vivek's curiosity at the coincidence drew him in. "Why do you like the mountains?" he asked.

"It's the solitude," the man said. "I love to be myself in the wilderness. When you're alone, you feel tremendous peace." He replied.

"Like the space between your thoughts," Vivek mused, reflecting on Amanda's words.

As the train came to a halt at Vivek's destination, he got up and said, "It was nice talking to you. Perhaps I will have the chance to travel to the Himalayas too." He felt guilty at saying this after just deciding not to meet Chidanandji at Gangotri.

The Scottish gentleman wished him a nice evening and unexpectedly presented him with the brown package. "I would like you to have this for your trip to the Himalayas," he said. Vivek was puzzled and taken aback at the same time; puzzled because he wondered if he should accept a package from a stranger and taken aback that the man would assume that he was traveling to the Himalayas.

As if sensing his apprehension, the man said, "Please, this is my gift to you. You'll find the information in it useful for your trip."

Vivek graciously accepted it as the man removed his glasses. Vivek was struck by his sparkling blue eyes. "Thank you. You're too kind," he said. "Now I will have to plan my trip. Have a nice evening." He exited the subway holding the strange brown package, wondering what was inside. Tucking it under his arm, he quickly made his way home.

When he got home, he noticed the blinking light on his phone, indicating four new messages. One was from his mother, another was from Greg and two were marketing calls. No message from Amanda. "Thank goodness," he thought. "She must have given up."

He was tired but still curious about what was in the package—presumably a book from the shape and size of it. He ripped it open and stared in disbelief at the contents.

The book was titled *The Source of the Ganges—The Gangotri*. The author's name was William Chadwick III. Vivek couldn't believe his eyes. As he flipped to the back cover he about fell over. There was his picture—the man from the subway with the sparkling blue eyes. He read Chadwick's bio. He was a professor of geology from King's College, London. He had traveled to the Alps, the Andes, and the Himalayas.

Shaking, Vivek set the book down and went over to his laptop. He quickly Googled Chadwick's name, but nothing came up. It appeared that he didn't exist. He went back to the book and took down the ISBN number and entered it into Amazon. Nothing came up again. It was as if the book and author didn't exist.

He opened the book again and searched for the publication date—February 23, 2009. The date was familiar, but why? Suddenly it hit him. What were the odds that Mr. Chadwick would have published the book on the day that he had first met Chidanandji in Thiruvannamalai? This was too much of a coincidence to be a coincidence.

He started leafing through the pages of the book, noting that it contained beautiful illustrations of the Himalayas and spectacular pictures of the Ganges, especially Gangotri. There was also a detailed write-up of the area and how to get there.

Just then, a business card fell out of the book. The whole room was filled with a jasmine smell mixed with rose—the signature fragrance of Chidanandji. Vivek picked up the card. It was colorful, with a picture of Gangotri and the Himalayan landscape. The only writing on it read: "Chidanand, Gangotri." Vivek's mouth fell open. He turned the card over and read a quote: "My miracles are my visiting cards. They beckon my devotees to me." A chill ran through his body.

He immediately picked up the phone and called Amanda. "Amanda, this is Vivek. Something utterly amazing has happened. I'm sorry for calling at this late hour, but can we meet ASAP?"

Amanda voice resonated across the phone. "Sure. You're welcome to come over here. I was waiting for your call." She gave him directions. Vivek quickly grabbed the book and card and headed out the door, forgetting to lock it behind him in his haste.

Chapter 8

Vivek drove like a maniac. When he arrived at Amanda's doorstep, it was almost midnight. As soon as he entered her apartment, he started telling her about the book and his serendipitous meeting with Chadwick on the subway. She took the book from Vivek and started leafing through the pages. She was also surprised to find no reference to it or the professor on the Internet. They both came to the unavoidable conclusion that Chidanandji had a hand in the chance encounter. He had materialized himself as Bill Chadwick III and the book on Gangotri. When Amanda checked with the Library of Congress two weeks later, after Vivek had left for India, about the ISBN number in the book, she discovered that it was one of the unused numbers in their catalog. Chidanandji had somehow known this and chosen to use this number for the book.

Vivek felt terrible for doubting Chidanandji and his authenticity. Amanda consoled him by reminding him that by him not choosing to go to Gangotri, he was able to witness the miracle of Chidanandji materializing before him.

Vivek pleaded with Amanda. "Please tell me how you came to know Chidanandji. Tell me everything you know about him."

Amanda's story started to unfold. "My parents met each other in London in their early twenties. My father, Jasbir Singh, had just finished his college degree. My mother, Anne Butler, was a school teacher. It was almost love at first sight when Jasbir went to meet the school principal for a job as a contractor (my grandfather was a builder) to build an extension to the school where my mom worked. He not only built the extra classroom, he also built their relationship. My mother loved Indian culture and Indian philosophy, though she'd been raised Catholic. My father respected Guru Nanak[25] but did not follow the dictums of being a Sikh. He did not sport a turban, long hair, moustache or a beard. He was a modern Sikh. After they got married, I was born two years later and his business doubled and tripled.

"They were excited by my arrival in the world, but little did they realize what was in store for them. I didn't learn to speak, play, or walk as a normal child, even after one year. I lay in a bed most of the time. And I didn't even seem to recognize my parents or the world around me. They thought that I was autistic or had a brain injury or a developmental problem.

"My parents became depressed and didn't know what to do to help me. My childhood was a lonely one. I didn't have friends. I looked normal on the outside, but was broken on the inside. But my parents loved me so much that they decided to take me to India—to the Vaishnavi Devi[26] temple in Kashmir to see if I could be healed by the power of the divine mother or the blessings of a spiritual master.

"For three months straight, they took me to the temple every day and prayed. But nothing happened. They gave up all hope. Dad went to Delhi to plan our return trip home to London and mom was walking back from the temple with me. Suddenly, a holy man in his fifties appeared and began speaking to her in English.

"He asked where she was from and she told him, and she explained why she was there with me. The holy man then told her that I had already been blessed. Then he asked her to give her child to him for a month so that he could make me a normal and healthy child. My mom was shocked and refused. The holy man understood and told her to check with my father and come back the next day to the same place at the same time. And he referred to my father by his name, which really freaked my mom out.

"Anyway," she continued, "Mom told Dad everything when he got back from Delhi that evening. My parents didn't know what to do. They didn't

25 Guru Nanak: The founder of the Sikh religion.
26 Vaishnavi Devi temple: Temple of the Mother Goddess in Kashmir, near Sri Nagar.

want to just hand me over to a stranger, but they also wanted, with all their hearts, to cure me.

"They did meet up with the holy man the next day. Understanding their agony over leaving me, he promised that my mom could stay at his ashram while I was being cured. Dad was instructed to go back to London and to come back in a month to take us home again.

"Apparently, from what my mom told me, the holy man poured so much love and affection on me that he literally willed me to be a normal child. Every day he would apply herbal oil all over my body, wrap me up in a woolen blanket, and sit in front of me and meditate for hours. Mom was amazed at the extraordinary love he had for me. Sometimes she could see tears streaming down his cheeks. As time passed I started developing normal capabilities. In three weeks, I started speaking and walking. After a month, it was as if I never had this disease. It was a miracle.

"Dad couldn't believe the transformation and my parents were eternally grateful. They accepted this holy man—and yes, you guessed it, the holy man was Chidanandji—as their guru. Then they were amazed all over again when Chidanandji explained what my problem had been all along."

Vivek's curiosity grew deeper with Amanda's story. "So what was it?" he asked with baited breath and complete concentration.

Amanda smiled and continued. "He told my parents that I had been a great yogin in my previous life and that Chidanandji and I had been fellow disciples to a great Mahatma[27]. We lived in that area thirty years ago and served our guru. The three of us were devotees of Vaishnavi Devi. Chidanandji referred to me as an elder sister who could grasp the deepest concepts of Adavitha much faster than he could. As part of our training, we learned to focus on the space between thoughts. From what Chidanandji said, I learned it instantly while he struggled with it." She paused with an amused look on her face. "I know what you're thinking. I too found it strange that I could reach spiritual milestones while he struggled.

---

[27]   Mahatma: Great Soul

"He went on to tell my parents that in our previous life, I would always meditate to the point of not eating, sleeping or being mindful of heat or cold. He used to force feed me. He was always so protective of me.

"I was a bit of stubborn spiritual being in my past life and wanted to experience ultimate bliss. I didn't want to be in my body anymore. I just wanted the truth. I was advised by my guru to not burn myself out and to lead a normal life. It wasn't supposed to be my decision, only the Almighty's decision. But being the stubborn person that I was, I did slip into a deep meditative state one day after I had manipulated Chidanandji to go get some fruit from the village, which was a two-day journey. My guru was also gone to help thousands of devotees throughout India, so I was all alone. Chidanandji had been told to keep an eye out for me, yet I was the one who deceived him in the end. By the time he came back, I was unconscious and couldn't be brought back. I became emaciated over the next several days and died.

"The deep meditational state I had gone into was dangerous and I didn't realize how dangerous it was until it was too late. Usually precautions are put in place when you go into deep meditation because parallel to the thought-force of the individual, there are corresponding cosmic forces of the world which are similarly governed by phenomenal laws. To create a blank state of the mind without safeguards, in the middle of the cosmos, is as dangerous as creating an unprotected vacuum in the midst of a high-pressure region.

"One has to train one's mind to adhere to thoughts relating to the ultimate truth. Otherwise, your mind is incapable of warding off other undesirable thoughts that might come in from the cosmic world, as well as the torrent of thoughts streaming in from all of your other past lives. Typical examples abound everywhere in the world. The presence of schizophrenics with multiple personalities in the Western world and the large number of people who are frequently possessed by ghosts and other beings in the Far East are such examples. Your mind can literally experience a meltdown, which is what happened to me. Chidanandji told my parents that I had been born again to get another chance to get it right.

"He told them that it was my destiny to be brought to the temple to be healed. He said that all he did to heal me was to apply the oil from the seed of my favorite fruit that I always asked for in my previous life and to stay with me to bring my attention back to the world.

"He also said that I would be a great exponent of Advaitha and that I was to be born in the Western world to learn the Western language so that I could teach the ancient truths to the modern man. Chidanandji is so sweet and loving. He thanked my parents for reuniting him with this beloved sister. He asked that they give me a Western education and that I attend Oxford and study Indian philosophy and Advaitha. He left them with the request that I come to him when I had finished my studies twenty years later."

Amanda had to laugh at Vivek's spellbound face. "So that's it in a nutshell." She shrugged.

Vivek couldn't believe what he had heard. It sounded more like a movie script than like someone's life. "So then what happened?" he asked.

"My parents brought me back to London, where I grew up as normal child," she replied. "They didn't talk about Chidanandji or show me any pictures of him, for fear that I would remember him and run back to India to seek him out. They needed to keep me focused on my studies until I was to meet up with him again in twenty years."

Vivek began to sound like a detective attempting to unearth clues to a puzzle. "Well, how did you find him, then, after all those years?"

Amanda grinned mischievously. "I'll tell you that story some other time. For now, we need to prepare you for your trip."

"When will you teach me how to focus on the space between thoughts?" Vivek persisted.

"That has to wait, too. Who knows, maybe Chidanandji will teach you that. As for trying to locate Gangotri, it's all in the book. In fact, the book is your road map for getting there. But I do have a request." She paused.

"Sure, what is it?" Vivek asked.

"Can I keep the book as a souvenir? We can always Xerox a copy of it for your trip."

"Sure," said Vivek. "But I'm still curious. Are you now able to experience the ultimate truth in meditation that you couldn't achieve in your past life?"

Amanda smiled. "No, not yet. But I'm sure that when the time is right, I will. For now, my job is to travel and teach others about Advaitha. Have fun on your trip. I'll come to the airport to see you off tomorrow."

Just then, Vivek's cell phone started playing Led Zeppelin. Vivek rolled his eyes. It was Greg Keaton again. He thanked Amanda for her help and support and made his way home. He couldn't help but think about her story and thought that she did indeed look like a goddess. It wasn't until he reached his front door that he realized that the fear he had felt earlier that day had been replaced with hope and joy.

Chapter 9

The following day was a hectic one for Vivek. He managed to get all his travel documents in time and make hotel reservations in New Delhi. By midnight, he was boarding an Air India flight that would take him on his journey. Dr. Amanda Singh and Greg Keaton saw him off at the airport as he patiently made his way through the security line. He waved goodbye to them and headed down the main terminal to his concourse where his flight—and his future, he felt—awaited him. Vivek patted the part of his backpack that held the Xeroxed copy of the book that Amanda had given him. Equipped with his road map and his curiosity, he felt ready to take a giant leap of faith and change the trajectory of his life forever.

Thankfully, the eighteen-hour nonstop flight from JFK to New Delhi was uneventful. He slept soundly through the whole trip due to the emotional upheaval of the past several days and awoke fresh and alert when they touched down. A limousine with a chauffeur from the Taj Hotel was waiting for him outside the airport. The plan was for him to stay at the Taj one day and leave for Rishikesh by taxi the next day. He had a reservation at a decent rest house at Rishikesh, but beyond that he had no idea what his itinerary was going to be except that he had to leave for Gangotri the next day, perhaps by car. He had been told he had to reach Uttar Kashi[28] in order to get to Gangotri. He was assured that there was a mountain road

---

[28] Uttar Kashi: A sacred city in the Himalayan ranges en route to Gangotri. The name literally means "North Kashi," in reference to the most sacred city in India, Kashi, at the banks of the Ganges (also known as Varanasi or Benares).

that went all the way to Gangotri, a drive that would take about twelve to fourteen hours.

He checked into his room at the Taj Hotel just before 4:00 a.m. It was the same suite he had booked the last time. After sleeping for three hours, he got up, showered, and was in line for the breakfast buffet by 8:00 a.m. He savored his breakfast and lingered over his coffee, since he didn't know when his next hot meal was going to be.

While he was eating his breakfast, his jaw almost dropped. There in the doorway were Vimalananda and Deepa Agarwal, the self-professed guru-makers from the scam class a few months before, entering the hall. Vivek was hoping that they would not see him, but unfortunately they sat down at a table right next to him. As Deepa looked around the room, her eyes fell on Vivek, and she blurted out, "Don't I know you? Weren't you in one of our seminars?"

Vivek nodded. At this, Deepa and Vimalananda gathered up their things and moved over to join him at his table. Amanda's warnings of spiritual masters as ego-gratifying entertainers echoed in Vivek's mind. Vimalananda was a businessman who undoubtedly could be extremely charming when he wanted something. "He's just like a management consultant," Vivek thought. "Full of himself, hot air, and his five affirmations."

After Deepa reminded him who Vivek was, Vimalananda said, "Hi, Vivek, how are you? Long time no see, buddy." He flashed his bleached set of teeth.

Vivek grimaced silently to himself at the malice hiding behind the mask of the false ego before him. "It's nice to see you again." He winced at the weakness of his words, and wished he could melt through the floor—but not before he finished his coffee.

Vimalananda kept up his marketing demeanor. "You have to see the new lesson plan. It is much better and much more student-friendly. You ought to see it."

Biting his tongue to keep from saying something that would deflate their egos, he replied, "I appreciate your offer, but I am not interested. I am pursuing another path of spirituality right now."

Vimalananda's white enameled teeth instantly disappeared behind pursed lips. His attempt to suppress his anger was not as successful as he might have liked. He clenched his fists and jaw and leaned forward to stare intently at Vivek. "I hope you don't find yourself following some other guru," he said, "especially not one like the one I used to follow, a fellow named Chidanand. He is an unscrupulous spiritual master, and there are others like him out there."

Vivek gathered that Vimalananda had fallen out of favor with the spiritual master and had gone his own way.

Vimalananda shook his head. "Vivek, let me tell you something. The Advaitha stuff is too dense for most people to fully comprehend. The program I have come up with is for the common man. In fact, I have a psychologist and psychiatrist from MIT on my team and they have entirely revamped the course."

Vivek was annoyed with Vimalananda's arrogance. He decided that there was no getting through to him and turned to Deepa as a last resort. "Deepa, I do not want to pick a quarrel. You follow your path and I will follow mine. Let us not drag Chidanandji into this."

He got up and abruptly left the marketing magnates to their meal. He had no more need of talking to the blind who had no eyes to see the truth.

A few hours later, he was en route to Rishikesh in an air-conditioned car driven by a chauffeur, not knowing what lay ahead of him. He was lost in his thoughts and hardly noticed the towns and the scenery as he passed by. The trip took all day and Vivek found himself dozing off from time to time. Before he knew it, day had turned to dusk; they had driven for over eight hours. The twilight sky transitioned to night as the sun descended beyond the hills. The twinkling stars began to dance against the black backdrop of the night sky as the car finally pulled up at the Travel Inn in Rishikesh at 10:00 p.m. Vivek got out, stretched his tired legs, rubbed his eyes, and yawned before gathering his luggage and strolling into the hotel lobby to check in. He retired for the night in a simple room with bare facilities. He had only brought along a backpack as his luggage and a small handbag that held his valet, passport, and the Xeroxed copy of the book on Gangotri. He had decided to leave his suitcase in the locker in the Taj Hotel back in New Delhi.

After a good night's sleep, Vivek got up at 4:00 a.m. He went for a walk along the banks of the Ganges and over to the Lakshman Jhula[29]. Very few people were around at that time. He had no clue as to what he was to do from there. The only thing he knew was that he had to be at Gangotri before the next night, which was also the full moon, Vaishak Poornima. He also knew that he could go by car from Rishikesh to Gangotri via Uttar Kashi in ten to twelve hours. He was planning to leave early the next morning by car, and meanwhile, he waited patiently for some sign of Chidanandji.

He visited the Shivananda Ashram and joined the worshippers. He came back to the room after lunch and was alone in his room for a long time. If he had to prepare for a car to take him to Gangotri he had to do it right away.

His attention suddenly shifted to a disturbance next door. He peered over his balcony into the balcony next door. Vivek's family was from Tamil Nadu and he could discern that the family having the discussion was from the same region. He recognized the dialect and gathered that they were business owners from Karaikudi[30]. There was a male servant who must have been the cook and a female servant who must have been taking care of the family's child. From their discussion, he was able to make out that they were returning after visiting the Mansa Devi temple at Haridwar.

The gentleman glanced over to Vivek sitting on a bamboo chair on his balcony and acknowledged him. He introduced himself as Arunachalam and his wife as Tamil Selvi and their six-year-old daughter as Mansa. Vivek tried conversing back in Tamil, but struggled with the dialect. Arunachalam instantly understood and switched to English.

Arunanchalam said, "You are welcome to join us for dinner." Vivek accepted—he was hungry and wanting some company. He quickly got ready and walked next door. Before he knew it, he was sitting at the table with the family while a servant brought out plates of food and drink. Vivek feasted on the rice cakes and lentil soup.

---

[29]   Lakshman Jhula: A swinging bridge across the Ganges in Rishikesh.

[30]   Karaikudi: A town in South India, inhabited by the Chettiar community, which later became a university town.

Arunachalam looked intently at Vivek as he chewed. He was curious as to why this American had journeyed so far away from home. "How is your new president Obama doing?" he asked in an attempt to initiate conversation at the dinner table.

Vivek wiped his face. "Well, America is slowly recovering under his leadership. Are you on vacation?"

"It's a long story, actually," Arunachalam replied, reaching for a second helping of dinner. "But I feel like telling it to you. You see, this is our daughter Mansa. She was a gift of God. After twenty years of marriage, we still had not been able to conceive a child. In desperation, I went to Gangotri to pray for a baby. I don't know how long I was praying, but out of blue, someone tapped me in the shoulder. I turned around and I saw the most benevolent holy man. He blessed me and gave me an apple. The funny thing was, he wasn't holding an apple when I first turned around. I don't even know where the apple came from. Anyway, he gave me this apple and said, 'Give this to your wife, Tamil Selvi. Next year she will give birth to a girl. Name her Mansa.' He then walked away. I was dumbfounded and wondered how he knew my wife's name. I literally ran back to Badrinath from Gangotri, clutching that apple."

Arunachalam shook his head, reliving the disbelief of years ago that miracles really could manifest themselves in people's lives. "Sure enough, my Mansa was born the next year. The day he gave me the apple was the Poornima day in the month of Vaishak. Since then, every year I have been coming to Gangotri, hoping to see the holy man and offer my gratitude to him. I will offer my entire wealth at his feet. But alas, I can't seem to find him. This year my wife insisted she would also come. We both want our daughter blessed by him, but we do not even know his name."

"I do," thought Vivek, for he was convinced that the holy man was none other than Chidanandji. His thoughts shifted when Arunachalam asked him what he was doing so far from home.

Vivek shrugged. "I am also looking for the holy man."

Arunachalam looked puzzled. "But how?"

"I'm supposed to meet with him before midnight tomorrow in Gangotri."

Arunachalam pressed Vivek for more information. "How are you getting there? Have you made plans?"

"Not yet." Vivek replied.

Arunachalam clapped his hands together. "Then don't plan. Come with us. We have lots of room in our van. Do you have a lot of luggage?"

"I only have a backpack." Vivek said.

"Good, then we will have plenty of room for our journey. We set out tomorrow in search of the precious sadhu[31]."

At the end of dinner, Arunachalam read off their itinerary, while referring to a map of the region. "We must leave early in the morning in order to get to our destination by dark. Uttar Kashi is 140 kilometers from here and Gangotri is 100 kilometers from Uttar Kashi. We will reach Uttar Kashi around noon. After a short lunch break, we will need to leave for Gangotri if we want to get there by five p.m." He suggested that they get a good night's sleep and assemble on the front porch at 5:15 a.m. Vivek graciously thanked his hosts for the meal and the opportunity to travel with them.

Later that night, he sat on his bed, amused by the synchronicity of the day's events. Within minutes, sleep overpowered him as he began dreaming of meeting up with Chidanandji again in Gangotri.

---

[31] Sadhu: Spiritual master or monk.

Chapter 10

Vivek was jolted awake by a loud knocking on his door. He had overslept. He looked at his watch and groaned—it was 5:05 a.m. Vivek opened the door a crack, squinted and told Arunachalam that he would be ready in a few minutes. The cold shower woke him up instantly and by 5:20, he was ready with his backpack. He climbed into the van with Arunachalam and his family. The cook gave Vivek a cup of hot coffee to wake him up a little more. Vivek gulped it and thought that it was one of the best cups of coffee he had ever had as he sat in the front seat next to Arunachalam, who had assumed the role of pilot of the expedition. His wife and daughter were in the middle seats, while the servants took up the rear. Vivek turned and said "Good morning" to the small band of travelers and then turned his attention back to the road. The engine of the van sputtered and groaned in the cold, releasing a puff of gas into the fresh morning air. After several powerful huffs and puffs it took off in its long trek towards Gangotri.

Although the road was designed for vehicles, it was also extremely narrow at times and treacherous to maneuver through. On more than a few occasions, Vivek said a little prayer in the hopes that his guardian angels and spirit guides would help him make it safely to his destination. At times, he was scared to look out the passenger window at the cliff dropping off below him as the van teetered on the edge of the barely manageable road.

The scenery, however, was spectacular. The road followed the landscape created by the Ganges River. At times, Vivek could see the river as it suddenly came into view and disappeared around the next bend. Sometimes the roar of the gushing water would be deafening, and at other times, it would sound like a distant murmur. It was almost as if the river were alive. The fragrance of the forest periodically changed from the fragrance of flowers to the fragrance of Deva Daru[32] trees to, at times, the unwelcome fragrance of animal and discarded waste from the thousands of travelers who traversed annually through the narrow passageways. Vivek cringed at the total lack of respect of humans towards nature and at the bundles of garbage strewn along the way and piling up on the side of the road in nauseating patterns. He murmured to himself, "Modern India will never learn the sanctity of cleanliness and respect due for Mother Nature." He reflected that the typical Indian attitude is that waste is someone else's problem, and was reminded of how people would sweep the area in front of their house, only to transfer the dirt to their neighbor's yard. In India, there was no ethic of civic responsibility for collective waste management.

Vivek felt the silence of Tamil Selvi from the back seat. He remembered Arunachalam bossing her around the evening before like a typical Indian husband, not trying to communicate with her. Strangely it did not seem to bother her. Vivek wondered if she had intellectual aspirations or if she was satisfied with her role as the mother. Her silence was a shroud that she hid behind where no one could reach her. Before he knew it, they had reached Uttar Kashi at fifteen minutes past twelve.

They stopped near a marketplace where the cook purchased some flatbread and potatoes to go with the yogurt rice and lemon rice that they had made and brought with them. The slight saltiness of the Indian potato chips married nicely with the alkaline creaminess of the yogurt rice. Compared to the tantalizing taste of the two, the flatbread was just that—flat—but not bad nonetheless.

After a brief rest, they started on the next phase of their journey to Gangotri. Gangotri sits at an altitude of about 10,000 feet, and as the van climbed, the road and the terrain became more difficult and the temperature dipped, while the scenery became more and more spectacular. They finally arrived at Gangotri at 5:30 p.m., some twelve hours after they had set out. Arunachalam found a rest house at Gangotri with crude facilities where they could stay. Once rested, the travelers decided to take a walk to stretch their legs and regain their circulation and to feel more alert.

---

[32] Deva Daru: *Cedrus deodara*, or evergreen tree of the Himalayas.

The River Ganga flowed with a tremendous force, speed and agility. It seemed to have the energy and force of a stampede of roaring elephants. Apart from the Ganges, the other major attraction was the temple dedicated to Mother Ganga, which had been constructed about a century earlier by a Rajasthani[33] king. This temple replaced the original temple, which had been there almost from the beginning of time, as legend would have it.

Due to the altitude and lack of oxygen, walking was difficult. Mansa was hungry and started crying. The walk was short-lived, as Arunachalam and his family and their tiny entourage of servants left to go back to the rest house to recuperate and to feed Mansa. Vivek continued to stroll along the river for some time, since the cottage was not far away and he could easily walk back.

He was hoping for a sign of Chidanandji to let him know that he was on the right path. He had done everything he could and here he was, in Gangotri on the banks of the river on Vaishak Poornima day. He started to feel vulnerable knowing that he was totally at the mercy of Chidanandji.

It was almost dark and he could see the full moon on the horizon. The roar of the Ganges nearby was deafening. Vivek looked at his watch. It was now 8:30 p.m. He had been sitting there on a rock at the edge of the river for more than two hours, lost in his thoughts and observing the people strolling by. There was still no sign of Chidanandji.

Another hour passed by. It was biting cold by now. There was hardly anyone on the road except for a few who were staying in tents on the banks of the river. Suddenly a fear gripped Vivek. What if Chidanandji did not keep his promise? What if he was left stranded? Arunachalam's cook had come by at least twice during the past three hours, saying that Arunachalam was worried about Vivek and asking why he had not come back to the rest house. Vivek assured him that he would come shortly and sent him back.

Vivek had lost all hope and was about to start his trek back towards the rest house. The brightly shining moon pierced through the night sky

---

[33] Rajasthan: Northwest province of India bordering Pakistan, famous for the valorous kings who fought heroically against the Mughals.

and hid occasionally behind a veil of clouds. The gentle breeze added to the wind-chill factor. Vivek shivered in his coat and wondered about his future. Suddenly, out of the corner of his eye, he caught a glimpse of a large procession of people coming from a distance. Vivek wondered what the commotion was about and noticed as they got closer that they were chanting prayers of devotion. In the middle of the throng was a holy man. In the moonlight, Vivek saw that everyone was eagerly looking at the man as they chanted, and that this man they were worshipping was blessing everyone.

As the group passed by Vivek, the saint turned and looked in his direction. In astonishment, Vivek jumped up and shouted, "Chidanandji, I am here!"

Chidanandji turned and acknowledged Vivek with a blessing and beckoned him to follow. The crowd split apart to give him room to get up next to Chidanandji, since the throng recognized the special bond between them. They all thought he must be someone very special for a saint to beckon him to his side.

The entire group went inside the temple. After a few minutes, Chidanandji approached Vivek and embraced him. "Welcome, my child. I was waiting for you for so many days. But first you must take me to Arunachalam's cottage. I need to bless Mansa. Poor Arunachalam has been coming to Gangotri every year for the last six years to see me."

Vivek laughed because only Chidanandji would know Arunachalam and his family and the real reason for their yearly journey. He could only imagine their joy and shock at seeing Chidanandji on their doorstep.

Chidanandji ended his prayer session and left with Vivek for the rest house. Vivek started shivering with cold in spite of his sweater. To his surprise, he saw that Chidanandji was only wearing a thick cotton robe and sandals. He showed no sign of being cold. They walked in silence until Chidanandji spoke up. "Vivek, I am glad you came. I know that Chadwick really annoyed you on the subway. How is Amanda? Isn't she a great soul? You must be very tired. You need rest. Sorry I made you wait in front of the Ganga Ma temple for several hours." Vivek tried to keep pace with Chidanandji's rapid change of thoughts.

By now they had reached the rest house. Chidanandji knocked on the door and gently called, "Arunachalam. I have come. Open the door." Arunachalam woke up, turned on the light and opened the door. He was in a total state of shock when he saw Chidanandji. His dream had been fulfilled. The person he had anxiously been searching for six years was standing on his doorstep! He shouted, "Tamil Selvi, Mansa! Come here. Guruji has come!" Then he broke down and sobbed for several minutes. Tamil Selvi and Mansa touched Chidanandji's feet and sought his blessings. Chidanandji patted Mansa affectionately on the head. He took Arunachalam and Tamil Selvi aside in a neighboring room and talked with them privately for fifteen minutes. Mansa was with Vivek. When they came out the eyes of both Arunachalam and Tamil Selvi were moist.

Chidanandji asked them to go back to sleep. He then turned to Vivek and asked, "Young man, can I share the room with you tonight?"

Vivek exclaimed, "Chidanandji, do you even have to ask?"

Chidanandji spread a sheet on the floor and immediately went to sleep in a savasana[34] posture. Vivek was lying close by in a sleeping bag. He could not believe his good fortune. Here he was sharing a room with Chidanandji. He wanted to tell Amanda how he was feeling. He felt as if he had known Chidanandji for a very long time. The whole room was filled with the aroma of jasmine and rose. He could hear the gentle breathing of Chidanandji amidst the sound of crickets outside the guesthouse. Slowly he drifted into the most peaceful sleep he had ever known.

---

[34]   Savasana: A yogic posture in which a person lies flat on the floor or bed as if he is dead, totally relaxing all the limbs of the body.

Chapter 11

Vivek was awakened by a gentle nudge. Chidanandji was up and ready to leave. He had smeared his forehead with vibudhi, a sacred ash. He looked like Lord Shiva[35]. Vivek looked at his watch. It read 3:45 a.m. Chidanandji whispered, "Vivek, go wash up. Get ready. Let us leave." Vivek was up and ready in a few minutes. He was excited and nervous at the same time. Grabbing his backpack, he gently closed the door behind him and followed Chidanandji outside. He could still hear the snoring symphony of the Arunachalam entourage in the next room. Chidanandji motioned for Vivek to be quiet while they slipped into the darkness preceding the light of dawn.

It was biting cold and Vivek was glad that he had the foresight to put on a thermal vest underneath his sweater, as well as his wool socks and hiking shoes. Chidanandi, on the other hand, only wore the same robe and sandals as before. Remarkably, it was as if the frigid temperature had no effect on him.

The whole town laid in a deep slumber. They could hear the roar of the Ganges and the chirping of the crickets. The night mist surrounded them. They briefly stopped in front of the temple, peered though the small opening at the locked iron gate, and offered their prayers before proceeding.

---

[35] Shiva: The god of destruction among the trinity of Hindu gods, Shiva is responsible for eliminating the evil tendencies in man.

Chidanandji strolled along the riverbanks with Vivek following behind him. After a few minutes, Vivek started feeling a little hungry. As if he could read his mind, Chidanandji stopped and picked the leaves of a plant on the river's shore and crushed them. He turned to Vivek, held out his hand and asked him to chew the leaves. Vivek gingerly put the leaves in his mouth, not knowing what they would taste like, but once he swallowed them, he was amazed that his hunger disappeared and that his body was starting to feel very warm, as if the blood vessels were working overtime to create energy and body heat. He no longer felt the frigid chill of the Himalayan wind.

The pair then began hiking the mountain along the riverbanks. Silence was their companion. Vivek was so much overcome with emotion and adrenaline that he kept following the energetic Chidanandji like a little kid trailing after a parent. He had a million questions on his mind, yet couldn't recall a single one. He drew his energy from the therapeutic Himalayan mountain air. In fact, he had never felt so alive in all of his life as he felt now. The trail, strewn with stones, became more difficult as they went on. From what Vivek could see, the river had swelled its banks at one time, dislocating rocks and washing away the passageway.

Moonlight illuminated their way, and the twinkling stars in the night sky formed a gorgeous backdrop to the beautiful landscape around them. Vivek glanced at his watch. It was now 4:50 a.m. They kept up their brisk mountain hike for another hour. Between labored breaths, Vivek noticed with curiosity that Chidanandji was climbing as if just strolling down a path—effortlessly. He wasn't breathing hard at all. In fact, he was humming to himself along the way, and seemingly had energy to spare. There was no sweat on his brow. How did he do it? "Perhaps he's so used to the climb that his body has adjusted," Vivek mused. Finally, they arrived at a plateau that must have been at least 11,000 feet above sea level. The air was thinning out the higher they climbed, making it that much harder to breathe. The sun was rising in the east, casting a golden glow across the entire vast mountain range. As the mist cleared, Vivek could see a town in the valley.

"The air is a little thin here," Chidanandji commented. "Not enough oxygen for one accustomed to living at sea level like you. Your body will have to become used to the limited oxygen of the high altitude of these mountains. Let us relax for a while so you can catch your breath."

Vivek was thankful for the rest. He was indeed feeling the crushing pressure in his lungs. Chidanandji then gave him more of the crushed leaves, which were to be his breakfast. Again, when Vivek swallowed the leaves, his hunger disappeared and his energy came back in full force. He set aside his backpack and studied Chidanandji.

"Chidanandji, I am honored to be here with you. Thank you for inviting me to visit with you and learn from you. Amanda speaks very highly of you, by the way."

"It's funny that you did not believe at first," Chidanandji said. "You fought all the way. You almost decided not to come, which would have been the greatest blunder of your life. It might have taken another thousand years and many, many more births for you to get another opportunity like this."

Vivek threw up his hands. "Okay, Chidanandji, I admit it. I was an idiot and didn't understand."

Chidanandji cast an amusing glance his way. "You were not just an ordinary idiot, but an unfiltered idiot. Do you know what 'idiot' means?"

Caught off-guard by the questions, Vivek hesitated before answering. "Well, I think I know."

Chidanandji continued. "A fool is one who commits an occasional or accidental mistake. But an idiot is one who makes the same mistake over and over." He paused and leaned over to put his face closer to Vivek's. "So what happens when you switch the third and the fourth letters of that word?"

Vivek looked puzzled. "What? I don't get it."

Chidanandji leaned back and laughed. "Do I have to explain everything in detail? Think about it: The third letter is 'i,' the fourth letter 'o.' If you swap them, it spells 'i d o i t,' or 'I do it.' So, anyone who thinks he or she can do it is an idiot."

"Oh." Vivek pondered on this for a moment before replying. "I think that modern society and our educational system teach us to be idiots. We are taught over and over again that if we put the intention out there, we can achieve anything we desire, that we can do anything."

"It's the ego at work doing its thing to perpetuate the survival instinct." Chidanandji said. "Education and the pursuit of intelligence simply strengthen this false belief. If one continually thinks that they can do anything, then what is there to learn?"

Vivek thought about this for a moment. "Yeah, you're right." He shifted his seat on the boulder he was sitting on. "Chidanandji," he continued. "I'm almost afraid to ask. Where are we going and when will we get there? And what will we do when we get there?"

Chidanandji's laughter echoed across the canyons. "There your brain goes again—afraid because it doesn't know the outcome of the future and has to predict what will happen so that it can prepare itself for survival." His laughter settled down before he uttered his next statement. "Tell your ego that it needs a time-out because it's too stressed out." He found this statement to be funny too and started laughing again. "Oh, that's good one." He said, "The ego needs a time-out because it's stressed out. I'll have to remember that one."

Vivek laughed at Chidanandji's observation. He seemed like a little kid at times despite being the venerable teacher and spiritual leader that he was. Apparently he didn't take life as seriously as the rest of human civilization.

"This is the problem with the modern man," he went on. "Always full of questions—'Why this?' 'Why that?' My goodness, how do you ever get anything done?"

"Are we not allowed to question the world around us in order to learn more?" Vivek asked, seeking the answer to his question about questions.

Chidanandji looked around him at the mountain range before he replied. "No, I did not say you should not be curious or ask questions. I am only challenging the reason you are asking the question in the first place. Many times the modern mind asks a question and doesn't even wait for an answer. It is ready with another question and another question and so on. Even if the answer comes back, the questioner is so busy asking questions he has no time to decipher the answers or no patience to understand even if she or he recognizes it. People who ask the tough questions are considered the smartest people. If you were really sincere about your questions, you would have waited for the answer before you switched over to another question."

"But Chidanandji, what if the answer comes back after a long time or in some cases never comes back?"

Chidanandji sat back on the boulder and shielded his eyes with his hand as he looked at the sun. "If you cannot afford to wait for the answer to a question, then it means that the question was irrelevant, unimportant or insignificant in the first place. That means you are not really sincere in knowing the answers to the question as well. This is the hypocrisy of thinking. We settle for quantity and not quality. Have you noticed? A child asks a thousand questions every day and doesn't wait for the answers most of the time, or is satisfied with a shallow understanding of the answer. This is like eating in a hurry. You do not digest the food and invariably it leads to indigestion."

"Chidanandji," said Vivek. "Are you trying to say that I am totally incompetent to learn anything? God has given me senses, an intellect and memory. How can I best put them to use to learn?"

"Sensory perception is not the problem," Chidanandji explained. "The problem occurs when the brain gets the information and transforms it into emotions and thought. If we weren't so attached to old habits, beliefs, perceptions or information coming into the brain through our senses, then we could truly view the world as an unattached, independent observer. That way, nothing in the world can bind us. It's the brain's survival instinct that messes everything up. And, of course, that's where our ego is."

"So how do we observe without the feeling like we're the observer?" Vivek prodded.

Chidanandji absent-mindedly chewed some leaves. "Vivek, you can see without seeing. You can hear without hearing. You can even think without thinking. You think you need the senses to perceive. You think you need the mind to think. But you don't. It's as simple as that. Life exists in a state of simplicity. Our minds make it much more complex than it needs to be. We don't need the senses to perceive or the mind to think."

Vivek's brain was struggling to wrap itself around the new enlightened concept. "You are shattering all my domains of knowledge and common sense. I see because I have eyes. A blind man can't see. A deaf man can't hear. A brain-dead man can't think."

Chidanandji looked at Vivek. "Tell me," he said, "in your dreams, are your eyes open or closed? Can you hear?"

"Yes, my eyes are closed," said Vivek. "But my eyes can't see my dreams. So I don't understand your question."

Chidanandji reassured him. "Don't worry. Ask all you want to ask. I won't get upset with you. But be sincere in your questions and thoroughly understand the answers before you jump to the next question. The answer can never be found in the same plane as the question itself. When you look from the next higher plane, the question disappears altogether.

"The mind is incapable of explaining itself in its own plane," he went on. "So in order to explain it, you must go to the plane of Consciousness. Looking from that vantage point, you see the mind with all its doubts and difficulties transformed into Consciousness. And nothing ever remains which needs to be explained. Did you ever notice that you have plenty of questions in a dream about a dream existence but that they become irrelevant when you wake up?" Chidanandji then began reciting a poem:

> "Observations come and go, but senses remain.
> Forms come and go, but seeing remains.
> Perceptions come and go, but consciousness remains.
> But what is beyond consciousness? No one knows."

"So it's all about awareness," Vivek reflected.

Chidanandji nodded. "Yes." He pointed to a location in a distant canyon. "See that village down there? That's Bhojwasa. From here, Gomukh[36], the

---

[36]   Gomukh: The very spot where the Ganges flows out of the Gangotri Glacier. "Gomukh" means "the face of a cow." In ancient days, the boulders used to look like the face of a cow.

source of the river from the Gangotri Glacier, is only four kilometers away. It will take two hours to climb up the mountain to reach there. After darshan at Gomukh, we will go to Tapovan, which is another four kilometers away, for an overnight stay. Are you now satisfied?" Vivek nodded. "So tell me, why is your backpack so heavy? Did you take all of your worldly possessions with you?"

Chidanandji opened Vivek's backpack to see what he had brought. He found thermals, underwear, sweaters, slacks, flannel shirts, and a shaving kit. But what caught his attention was the Xeroxed copy of his book. He pulled it out and started leafing through it.

"Hmm, this is good book, if I do say so myself," he said. "I would like to meet the author sometime." He chuckled at his own joke before tucking the book back into place.

"Okay, okay, enough of this nonsense," he said. "We should get going. Give me your backpack. It is too heavy for you to carry for the rest of the climb. I will send it by post ahead of us."

Before Vivek could object, Chidanandji hurled the bag into the valley below. Vivek shouted, "Chidanandji, I need those things!" With dismay, he watched his bag drop like a rock. In the distance below, it just seemed to float on the river before it disappeared from view. Vivek groaned. There went the clothes that he would need for the rest of his trip. "I hope he can materialize a fresh set of clothes for me," he thought and glanced at his watch. He was shocked to see that it was already 10:10 a.m. "Where did the time go?" he wondered.

Suddenly a group of villagers appeared from behind the trees. They approached Chidanandji reverently and touched his feet. Chidanandji was overwhelmed with bliss to see them, as if he were greeting long-lost relatives. He talked to every one of them in what seemed to be a Tibetan or Nepalese dialect, undoubtedly inquiring about their families and their spiritual practices.

They offered him flatbread, lentils and rice. Chidanandji tasted the food and ordered Vivek to consume it all. Vivek's hunger had returned and he gulped down as much as he could. The villagers were amused at Chidanandji mimicking the way that Vivek was eating, since he wasn't used to eating with his bare hands. Chidanandji then spoke in Hindi, which Vivek barely understood.

"*Ab hamara chance. Kooch kilayenga.* Now it is my turn. I will feed you."

He asked Vivek to keep his palms open and together. Chidanandji placed his right hand over Vivek's, and hot, fresh, delicious-smelling laddu (sweet lentil balls broken up in loose form) fell in a seemingly never-ending flow into his hands. Vivek gave the food to the villagers, and they gratefully accepted it and ate. Vivek's hand was dripping with the ghee (clarified butter) with which the divine laddu must have been cooked. Chidanandji's right hand was spotless.

After finishing their meal, Chidanandji and Vivek bid goodbye to the villagers. After a steep climb through windy forest paths, Vivek could at last see Gomukh at a distance. The scene was awesome. He saw up ahead the Gangotri Glacier with huge ice boulders spread across it. Vivek had never seen anything like it in his life. He looked down and saw the Ganga flowing in all its glory. The sun was close to its zenith, blazing against the backdrop of the mountain, its light cascading off of the upper edges of the glacier. It was a once-in-a-lifetime experience.

Chidanandji took a handful of the Ganges water and sprinkled it on himself and Vivek. The roar of the mighty river was deafening.

"We will come back here after a few days," he said. "Inside this huge mountain there is a vast cavern. The Ganges drops from the top of the glacier mountain, and becomes a massive waterfall, with a vertical drop of at least two thousand feet inside the mountain. Humanity does not yet know about it. I myself have only seen it once. After a week at Tapovan I am going to take you there. I called you for this unique fortune to be bestowed on you. This place is filled with such heavenly vibrations; worldly-minded people cannot withstand the divine power even for a few seconds without becoming unconscious. If I took you now, you would die. I have to prepare you over the next week for this unique journey. I have not shown this place to anyone, including Amanda. It is your greatest fortune that has earned you this merit. Your scientists and geologists don't even know about this. It may take sophisticated instruments to detect the Bhageeratha cave which is buried a thousand feet inside the glacier. And it may very well be that the Divine will not permit them to see it, lest they destroy its natural beauty."

Vivek was too numb to even react. He couldn't believe what he was seeing and experiencing. The scenery was absolutely spectacular—too incredible to be true. He felt like pinching himself to see if he was dreaming or not. He continued to follow Chidanandji in a daze toward Tapovan. He began to stumble as he hiked. The thin air, exhaustion, and overwhelming adrenaline rush were too much for him. He felt only semi-conscious. Chidanandji turned around and stopped. He held Vivek's hand and muttered something.

Vivek closed his eyes and instantly felt as if he and Chidanandji were floating in the air. He thought he was hallucinating. After a few moments, he heard Chidanandji whisper in his ear, "Vivek, wake up. We have reached Tapovan." When he opened his eyes, he found himself lying in front of some huts. He abruptly sat up and noticed that he had somehow been moved to a snowy valley. Even more shocking was that his backpack lay next to him—the same backpack that Chidanandji had tossed down into the Bhojwasa valley several hours earlier. An incredulous smile spread across Vivek's face.

Chapter 12

As Vivek discovered, Tapovan is one of the most serene places in the world. He knew that for millennia, many spiritual masters had used it as a summer abode for undisturbed contemplation. The air itself seemed to be electrified with the energy of the Divinity. There were multiple ashrams close to one another there, and the scenery from each house was spectacular. Tapovan lay at the base of the Shivaling[37] Peak, which shone brilliantly as if cast in gold during sunrise and sunset. The entire area, blanketed by the eternal snow of the Gangotri glacier, was spectacular, calming even the most turbulent of minds. The landscape was littered with occasional bodies of snowmelt from the hot sun, with rivulets and some patches of greenery, flowers, and shrubs.

Chidanandji was the most respected celebrity among the spiritual masters there. Vivek and Chidanandji, meanwhile, were to share a rudimentary hut. Vivek was given instructions on the daily schedule that he was to follow. He was to rise at 3:00 a.m. for an exhilarating bath in a nearby hot spring, come back to the hut, and then attend a three-hour awareness session from 4:00 a.m. to 7:00 a.m. Chidanandji had transcended the duality of sleep and wakefulness—as he already existed in the highest state of bliss, his body did not need to sleep. However, he would adhere to the same schedule he had dictated to Vivek as an example for him to follow.

---

[37] Shivaling Peak: The glacier mountain which resembles a shivalinga, an oval-shaped stone, a symbol of the formless god.

At 7:00 a.m., spiritual aspirants from the neighboring area came to deliver a hot bowl of goat's milk from the special kind of sheep that lived in the area, along with dried fruits and nuts. This was followed by a discussion with Chidanandji every day from 8:00 a.m. to 11:00 a.m. About twenty to thirty sadhus (spiritual masters) and some local villagers from Bhojwasa and other places also attended these sessions. At 11:30, they sat down to a simple lunch of parathas and dhal (wheat bread and lentil stew), and occasionally, they received a bowl of rice with yogurt, which the villagers might have brought from the plains along with fruits.

The entire village rested from 1:00 to 3:00 p.m. Chidanandji, however, not needing any sleep, either read the scriptures, edited his works for publication, or responded to letters and queries from all over the world. Upon awaking at 3:30 p.m., Vivek was served a hot cup of tea.

A devotion session ran from 4:00 p.m. to 6:00 p.m. each day, followed by a snack of light sacramental food (nuts and fruits) and, if they were lucky, a glass of hot cow's milk. This was then followed by another awareness session from 7:00 p.m. to 10:00 p.m.

This routine went on for seven days. By now, Vivek had totally immersed himself in the simple and spiritual culture of the mountain people. He had even forgotten about his Blackberry and iPhone, which had died long ago. Only his Rolex watch survived the extreme weather conditions and continued to display time correctly and was the only tie he had to the so-called civilized world and his old life. Some days it was cold and other days comfortably warm around noon. Vivek enjoyed most of the intense and long awareness sessions in the morning and the evening and also the discussion sessions with Chidanandji.

Miracles happened every day in the presence of Chidanandji, including the transformation of Vivek's turbulent mind, once distracted by the materialistic pursuits of the Western world and civilized society, to a peaceful state of consciousness and awareness. He was being prepared for entering the Bhageeratha Ghufa, the sacred cave inside the Gangotri Glacier near Gomukh.

Vivek loved to observe the discussion sessions between the spiritual masters and Chidanandji. The masters were encouraged to ask him questions. One day, Vivek was part of a discussion that began with a sadhak[38] asking, "Chidanandji, we all know what the right thing to do is. We have heard you so many times. Yet circumstances sometimes prevent us from doing the right thing. Why is that?"

Chidanandji replied, "An emotional spike is needed to transcend the current limited existence. It can happen through deep depression, desperation or extreme happiness. I don't care how much money you have or how depressed or desperate you are, you can still point your mind in the right direction of consciousness because it is only there that you will truly be eternally free."

Vivek spoke up and said, "But Chidanandji, there seem to be so many obstacles."

Chidanandji went on, "To the most spiritually inspired, there is no obstacle. You choose to be happy or not happy. A wise person is happy for no reason. An unwise person is unhappy for no reason. That is the only difference between a wise and an otherwise person."

A sadhu[39] spoke, saying, "But we are beset with so many desires. Initially we have desires of the body. Slowly these are replaced by the desires of the mind, and then the desires of the intellect. A man who was a millionaire and renounces everything to become a spiritual master eventually becomes even attached to his kamandalam[40] and sleeping mat. It is only a change of scenery, but the emotions, uncertainties and the vacillations remain the same. Does praying to God help?"

Chidanandji replied, "The answer is yes and no."

The assembly was shocked by this answer. Everybody knew prayer always helped. The sadhus looked at one another and a voice piped up in the room: "If prayer does not help, then what else will help? Why should we pray?"

---

[38]   Sadhak: An aspirant in the spiritual path.
[39]   Sadhu: Monk.
[40]   Kamandalam: Portable water pot.

Chidanandji went on, "You approach God to fulfill your desires, one after another. You develop confidence and you trust God more. This is the good consequence of prayer. Man invokes in his prayer his own inborn power to cure, to create a miracle. He attributes the power to a God outside himself, and becomes a slave to fulfilling his prayers rather than recognizing the divinity within that makes this possible. He depends more and more on the outside influence of God to fulfill his desires. This eventually cuts at the root of his self-dependence and self-confidence, and makes him weaker and weaker day by day until at last he becomes helpless and passive, without any power of initiative. He focuses on the next prayer he wants fulfilled, rather than on the power of divinity that can fulfill all his prayers and take him beyond prayers." Chidanandji then recited a poem:

> "You pray so that you don't ever have to pray.
> You read so that you don't ever have to read.
> You meditate so that you don't ever have to mediate.
> You seek the help of a guru so that you don't ever have to need a guru.
> You realize so that nothing of yourself is left anymore."

"Everything is just an instrument to be used and then discarded," he concluded.

The sadhu said, "That seems to be a selfish approach. Where is gratitude?"

"You use one thorn to remove another embedded in your foot," said Chidanandji. "Do you then feel grateful enough to put the thorn that helped you back into your foot?"

Vivek couldn't help objecting. "You shouldn't just discard your spiritual master. That's not respectful."

What Chidanandji said next sent shock waves around the room.

"Actually, yes it is. Once they serve their purpose, discard them."

Chidanandji abruptly got up and signaled that the discussion was over for the day. There was a great commotion among the crowd, and even Vivek was very confused.

Vivek silently followed Chidanandji to their hut. He couldn't rest because his thoughts were entangled in the discussion that had just taken place. He also had more than enough energy to last a lifetime, so he decided to distract his mind by organizing and responding to Chidanandji's mail. Chidanandji had already written the answers to the questions people had sent him and Vivek's job was to write the reply on behalf of Chidanandji in stylized cursive script. He also read through the partially completed chapters of Chidanandji's monumental work on Advaitha, *Advaithamrutham: The Nectar of Adavitha.*

Vivek and Chidanandji did not speak to each other for the rest of the day. The silence was accompanied by the beautiful singing and music of the villagers and visitors.

After the evening meditation Vivek tried to sleep but couldn't. Chidanandji's words kept running through his mind. "Why am I here?" he thought. "If I have to eventually discard Chidanandji, then why make contact in the first place? What a waste of time and energy."

He looked over and saw Chidanandji lying flat on the ground in sublime sleep. The hut was filled with the scents of jasmine and rose. Vivek tried to sleep flat on the floor, but couldn't. "How does he do it?" he thought as he tossed and turned all night. When 3 a.m. rolled around, he groaned. He had not slept a wink.

Chapter 13

The next day at Tapovan dawned as every other day. It was bone-chilling at 3:00 a.m. and the bath at the hot springs was not as enjoyable as it had been on the other days. Chidanandji had not spoken a word to anyone, including Vivek, since the discussion of the previous morning. He seemed neither serious nor upset. His face was serene, but he did not seem interested in any conversation. The morning awareness session was a washout for Vivek. He was still disturbed by Chidanandji's comments from the previous day, and very tired. Chidanandji acted as if nothing had happened. They had a quiet breakfast of fruits and nuts and were fortunate to get a glass of hot cow's milk. Someone must have brought it from the plains the previous night. They were also given small quantities of sweet puffed rice. It tasted delicious, but in that moment, Vivek's tongue longed for the salt, potato chips, and French fries of his Western diet.

Everyone assembled for the morning discussion earlier than usual. They were anxious to find out more about discarding spiritual masters and curious as to what Chidanandji was going to say to explain his statements from the previous day.

Chidanandji sat silently with his eyes closed. It was a tense moment. Ten minutes passed. Twenty minutes passed. There was no sign of Chidanandji opening his eyes. Finally, at 10:30 a.m., there was movement. Chidanandji abruptly got up and went to his hut. Vivek got up and followed him nervously. Everyone felt that they had done something grievously wrong to upset Chidanandji. He had never abandoned his customary discourse or discussion during his summer stay at Tapovan.

As Vivek followed Chidanandji into the hut, Chidanandji spoke for the first time in twenty-four hours.

"Vivek, pack your bag and leave. You are not yet ready for this. I do not want to see your face when I come back." He darted out of the hut and disappeared in the distant landscape.

Vivek was totally devastated. He did not know what to do. He had never faced anything like this in his life. Throughout his entire life, he had always been in the driver's seat. Now, for the first time, he felt the rug being pulled out from under his feet. Here he was, in a distant and unfamiliar land and not in control of his life. And here he was, too, at the mercy of Chidanandji, who had just reprimanded him and ordered him to leave as if he were punishing a child for acting up. He felt angry, deceived, and, above all, insulted.

The sages and other senior devotees advised him to pack his bag and not go anywhere, but to wait in the hut until Chidanandji came back. They each recounted many such instances when Chidanandji had become angry but had eventually cooled off and forgiven the person he was upset with. Vivek waited all day but there was no sign of Chidanandji. He was feeling guilty. He really didn't know what he had done wrong, except for disapproving of Chidanandji's comments from the day before.

Chidanandji did not attend the evening awareness session either. Vivek even slept alone in the hut that night, anger replaced by worry about Chidanandji. At 3:00 a.m., he bathed in the natural spring as usual, and as he got out, he was startled by the noise of an animal. Vivek instantly sprung out of the pool as a huge snow leopard jumped into it. Shocked, he witnessed Chidanandji running after it as if he were a young man full of strength and stamina. Chidanandji stopped at the edge of the pool, where the large cat leapt out, circling him before stopping to lick his toe as if it were a pet. Chidanandji patted the dripping animal, and then noticed Vivek. He straightened up and shouted, "Why are you still here? Did I not ask you to leave?"

Vivek was still taken aback by what he had just seen. "Everyone said I should wait until you come back."

Chidanandji's tone was still fraught with anger. "Do you listen to me or to them?"

"Chidanandji," Vivek implored, "I don't want to leave. I want to be with you. Please forgive me for whatever I have done. I shouldn't have criticized what you said. Whatever you say must be true. I am just new to this surrender thing."

Seeing Vivek's plight and helpless pleading, Chidanandji's face lit up with a huge smile. He laughed a deep belly laugh, which resounded across the valley. Vivek was taken aback by the abrupt change in temperament and couldn't help but wonder if the almighty Chidanandji was a bit bipolar. Chidanandji strolled over to Vivek, patted his shoulder and started walking back to the hut with him with the leopard stealthily following in the shadows. The few villagers milling around at that time of the morning when night gently rolls into daybreak didn't seem fazed by the snow leopard. Once inside the hut, the large cat sat next to Chidanandji, rubbed his giant head against his legs, and started purring.

Chidanandji gazed at Vivek. "Do you know why I asked you to leave yesterday?"

Vivek shrugged. "I thought that you were upset with me because I was not a good listener."

"No, that's not the reason." Chidanandji then opened his hand and a tag fell to the ground. Vivek picked it up. It was a visitor tag from a New York hospital. The name on the tag read Sid. He gave Chidanandji a puzzled look. "What's this?" he asked.

Chidanandji fondly petted the leopard that had gone to sleep at his feet. "Yesterday your mother had a heart attack at home while she was praying to me. At first I thought I was going to send you there, but then I decided to visit her myself. I also wanted to shake you a little bit to test whether you are ready for the next phase of your spiritual life. When I went there as a visitor they asked my name. I said Chidanand. The nurse didn't understand and wrote Sid instead."

"Oh, my God," Vivek cried out. "Is my mom okay? She's not going to die, is she?" Immediately he was submerged in guilt knowing that he was the cause of the stress that had led to her heart attack.

Chidanandji waved his hand in reassurance. "Don't worry. She's okay. In fact, she'll be discharged in a few days. I blessed her and told her not to worry about you. I told her you are my child. She is peaceful now." Chidanandji smiled, "And she hasn't given up on arranging a marriage for you." Vivek groaned and rolled his eyes.

Chidanandji continued, "She pleaded with me to help you find a good woman to marry. I gave her my word that I would not force anything on you and that you were totally free to make your own decision."

"Thanks." Vivek said. "Maybe that'll get her off my back about this whole marriage thing."

Chidanandji then told Vivek to rest until the morning discussion at 8:00 a.m. "You look tired. You need some sleep." He sounded like a doting parent.

By the time of the 8:00 a.m. session, the entire town was assembled and waiting. Everyone was curious to know what had happened to Chidanandji.

A sadhu began the discussion by saying, "Chidanandji, you shocked us by disappearing yesterday. We thought that we had done something wrong and were taken aback by your statement about discarding our spiritual masters once they're no longer needed. We're feeling more confused than ever."

Before answering, Chidanandji motioned for Vivek to come and sit in the front with him. Vivek approached as Chidanandji addressed the crowd. "Dear friends, you are struggling with the concept of thought as reality. First of all, everything you claim to see, hear, or touch is nothing more than your own thoughts. For instance, you say you love someone. But love is a thought. And a thought cannot really interact with matter. So therefore, a thought is not real. That's why Advaitha declares that the world is unreal, because thoughts are unreal since they are fleeting and change all of the time.

"In a similar manner, your idea of a spiritual master and your love for this person is just a thought. It's not real. You think it is, because your mind deceives you into thinking that it's real, but it's not. That's why so many people are disillusioned when a spiritual master disappoints them. They thought that they were going to be a certain type of person and they weren't. Again, it was all based on a thought that was fleeting.

"So what we tend to do is to replace one thought with another. But a chain is always a chain. You become a prisoner of the chain of your thoughts. The ultimate goal is to break the chain and transcend your thoughts. Again, thoughts are only temporary and need to be discarded so that you can transcend to a state of consciousness where thoughts are not welcome. Awareness and thoughts cannot coexist.

"Spiritual masters are teachers. And there are many teachers at different stages of our lives—parents, educators, spiritual guides, etcetera. There are also two kinds of teachers: those who set an example of what to do and those who set an example of what not to do. In that sense, we are fortunate. A large majority of people are setting an example of what not to do. And still we do not learn.

"So when I said you should discard even your spiritual teacher, what I really meant was that you should discard your thought impressions of your guru and his teachings, and instead build your own self-confidence. You think I will be happy if you flatter me, if you mimic me, or if you respect me. Nothing could be farther from the truth. I will be happy only if you are peaceful and happy by yourself, without any support or help from me."

The throng in the room began to absorb Chidanandji's words. Now it made sense. Chidanandji suddenly got up, signifying that the morning discourse was over. Everybody was quiet. Vivek was tremendously impressed. He silently followed Chidanandji to the hut.

The rest of the day was spent in silence. Chidanandji spent the evening leafing through some scriptures. At night, the spiritual master went out and stared at the brilliant sky ablaze with thousands and thousands of distant planets and galaxies. There was no other place on earth that matched the beauty of the Himalayan sky. Stars danced against the deep darkness of the night sky.

As Vivek was about to fall sleep, Chidanandji told him matter-of-factly, "Be prepared. Tomorrow I am going to teach you how to focus on the space between thoughts so that you can go to the Bhageeratha Ghufa in a few days. You can go to this sacred spot if—and only if—you can master this."

With that, Chidanandji went abruptly to sleep. Vivek sat motionless, his heart palpitating. The pressure was on and he felt like he was facing college finals to graduate. It seemed his prayer was going to be answered at last. He kept staring at one of the brightest stars through a small opening in the hut until the goddess of sleep overpowered him.

Chapter 14

Excitement could be felt around the room at the next morning's discussion. There were more questions hanging in the air.

A sadhak asked, "Chidanandji, I don't seem to be making much progress with my spiritual development. I'm more confused than ever. Sometimes I feel like quitting."

Chidanandji replied, "Your state of mind is understandable during the first ten years of your spiritual journey. It is even understandable during the next ten years after that. But you've been at this for thirty years now and should have progressed. Now you need to look within and identify what your problem really is. Maybe you're worrying too much.

"Being in the present moment is the greatest antidote for worries. Worries are nothing but thoughts of the past or of the future. So worries are not real, either—just like thoughts. You feel guilty for not moving forward because you're too focused on the past. Every moment in time is a fresh start, so forget the past and get over yourself." Laughter erupted in the room.

The sadhak went on, "I get it, but even after having you as my teacher for thirty years, I still haven't transformed."

"According to the great sage Adhi Shankara[41]," said Chidanandji, "there are three rare boons that can be attained only through divine grace: to be born as a human, to come into contact with a sage or God himself, and to desire liberation.

"Having been born as a human, and having come into contact with a great teacher is not enough. You also need to have a burning desire to realize your true self. When your yearning is deep enough, a teacher will come into your life. You will then be gradually taken to the higher states of consciousness. Eventually you will hold onto only one desire, and that is to become desireless.

"The only way to overcome misery is to rise above it. You cannot continue to dwell in misery and yet hope to be unaffected by it. Feeling miserable is just a sequence of thoughts. Get over it. Saying that you are rich, poor, weak, or strong are just thoughts and nothing else. Labels are thoughts. Judgments are thoughts. And thoughts are not real. In the morning you were happy, at noon you were serious and at night you were sad. The only common thing between these three experiences is the 'I' and not the feeling of happiness, seriousness, or sadness.

"Even as you enjoy the world around you, it is your own real nature of peace that you experience as happiness. For example, you enjoy happiness listening to sweet music. Here music helps you only to empty your mind of

---

41   Adhi Shankara: A great sage and philosopher who lived a millennium ago. By the age of five he renounced the world and become a monk. By the age of sixteen he had composed some of the greatest commentaries on Indian scriptures, especially the Bhagavad Gita (Song Celestial), the Brahma Sutra (The Aphorisms on the Absolute) and the Upanishads (the greatest philosophical treatises of India), and his works were referred to as Shankara Bhashya or Shankara's commentary or exposition. He traveled the length and breadth of India four times before he attained Maha Samadhi (Final Emancipation) by the age of 32. He popularized the Advaitha (Nondualism) philosophy and established four mutts (learning centers) at the four corners of India. Many consider him to be an incarnation of Shiva due to his monumental accomplishments. It is due to Shankara's brilliance that Buddhism and Jainism almost became part of mainstream Hinduism, and only pockets of believers in these religions remain in India after Shankara's advent.

all thoughts other than music, and until finally it is emptied of the thought of music also. Thus, the mind ceases to be and you become happiness, and that is your real nature.

"But if you cannot exist without an iPod, iPhone, iPad, Facebook, or Google, then it is not an enjoyment but an obsession. These are only distractions to your thoughts. It is the nature of the mind and ego to be greedy. By desiring too much, your ego destroys what is yours to enjoy. It is wrong to believe that the happiness comes from music, because music doesn't make you happy—you're only happy when the music deletes the thoughts and eventually the music itself goes away. Music is like a bridge that takes you from thoughts to happiness, but it is not happiness itself."

Another devotee said, "I can grasp what you are saying, but I have a hard time turning off my thoughts. Do you have any suggestions?"

"Let me tell you a story which will address this concern of yours," said Chidanandji. "There was once a sadhu. His name was Swami Confusananda. He was called Confusananda because he was such a remarkable individual with such a great gift of gab that he confused anyone who came in contact with him. He was so sharp and smart that if anybody talked with him for a few minutes, that person was confused for the whole day. If anybody talked with him for an hour, they were confused for weeks. If anyone stayed with him for a day they were confused for their entire life. Such was his power of confusion. Since he was a masterful orator, he became very popular. People started flocking to listen to him and he continued to confuse the heck out of everyone.

"One day, a reporter came to interview him. He wanted to know the secret of his success. Here's how the interview went:

Reporter: Swamiji, what is the secret of your success? Why are people attracted to you like bees? What is the source of your popularity? What is your mission? Why this obsession with confusion?

Confusananda: I confuse people to wake them up and help them find happiness. I find that people are too focused on one belief or idea or another that they start to judge others as not worthy. It happens not only on an individual level, but affects societies and civilizations, too. Self-righteous people are selfish people. There is more harm than good that comes out of focused thoughts; like greed, violence, anger, etc. So, by confusing everyone, I destabilize their cohesive thinking so they don't hurt each other anymore. By confusing them, I shake them out of their foundational beliefs and principles and wake them to the reality of uncertainty, chaos and unpredictability. They learn to laugh and have fun again. This is the reason for my success.

Let me introduce my prime disciple, Argumentananda. This fellow is so arrogant and annoying. Sometimes even I wonder why I keep him with me. He has no beliefs or loyalties to any single idea or thought. He truly believes in Newton's third law: Every action has an equal and opposite reaction. Hence, no matter what anyone says, he will take the opposite viewpoint and shake the very foundations of your confidence. This fellow argues and argues until he succeeds in confusing or angering everyone. He is like a robot with no heart. Even I do not know how to stop him once he gets started. For instance, if you say 'I want to pray to God,' he will ask, 'Who is God?' If you say, 'God helped me out of this situation,' he will bring up another situation where God apparently did not help you. He is prodigious in his memory and tenacious in his antics.

If by any chance Argumentananda fails, then I bring in my next disciple, Insultananda. This fellow is so obnoxious that it only takes him a few seconds to insult anybody. He will hit you with such force that you won't even recognize what hit you. If you say, 'I am a fan of healthy diets,' he will immediately assault you by saying, 'Is that the reason why you are so fat?' If you say that you like to sing, he will retort, 'With your coarse voice?' What Argumentananda cannot accomplish, Insultananda will do by eroding the confidence of the person.

And if Insultananda fails, I let loose Depressionananda. He can depress anybody in one minute. He knows exactly the right thing to say to depress you. If you say that the financial crisis is over, he will say, 'You ain't seen nothing yet. A bigger crisis is just around the corner.' If you say, 'I just turned sixty,' he will list dozens of diseases that can strike you in an instant and point out how vulnerable you may be. As soon as he sees you, he will say, 'Is everything OK with you? You seem to be depressed.' If you say, 'I feel fine,' he will reply, 'No, no, trust me, something is definitely wrong with you.' He will start every sentence with a "No, no, that can't be.'

Finally, if all three fail, my favorite disciple, Flatterananda, will come to my rescue. Sometimes when he talks to me, I myself feel so flattered that I am no longer sure whether he is telling the truth or pulling my leg. I have yet to see a human being who is flatter-proof. Suppose you tell someone that they sang well or spoke well. They will immediately say, 'No, no, it is not me. It is all God's grace.' Translated, that means 'It really is all me, me, me, but for the sake of politeness I am giving credit to God.' Flatterananda will find some way to flatter you within a matter of seconds. If you complain that your hair has turned gray, he will say, 'You look majestic and wise.' When Flatterananda is finished with you, you will be confused beyond imagination."

Chidanandji ended his story and paused, looking around the room before going on. "The reason this story strikes a familiar chord with us is that inside every one of us, there is this Confusananda and his disciples Argumentananda, Insultananda, Depressionananda, and Flatterananda. So long as we are under their influence, we can never progress." He focused his gaze on the questioner in the room. "This is the reason why you feel depressed and have not progressed in spite of following the spiritual path for over thirty years."

At this point, Chidanandji stopped talking and waved his hand. A huge color poster suddenly materialized in it. Though many people in the group were fluent in Hindi and other regional languages, Chidanandji had produced this poster with English captions for the sake of Vivek.

Chidanandji pointed to the poster, saying, "There are nine stages in the spiritual journey from ignorance to illumination." Then he started describing each one.

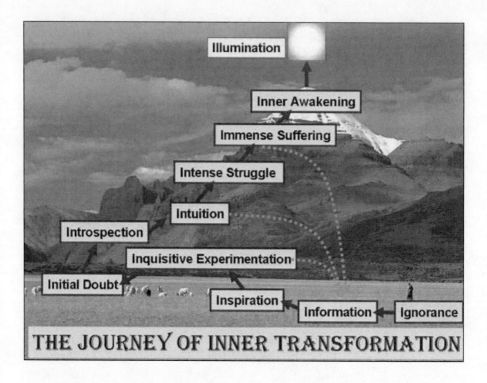

THE JOURNEY OF INNER TRANSFORMATION

"See the Mount Kailash[42] in the picture above," he said. "The peak represents **Illumination,** the goal of all aspirations. However, one has to start from the plains, in the current stage of **Ignorance**. The process is almost the same whether it is a spiritual quest or a pursuit of worldly excellence. First we seek **Information**, which hopefully will lead us to **Inspiration**. In our enthusiasm, we embark on **Inquisitive Experimentation**. However, since this constitutes our first attempt, it invariably leads to **Initial Doubt,** which necessitates the need for more information, and the cycle continues, until one converges on some basic beliefs and operating principles.

"Then the effort becomes steadier but leads to **Introspection** (self-audit) and is fueled by **Intuition** (inner promptings). At each of these stages, one is liable to fall back into the earlier stages and needs to climb up the mountain again and again. Eventually the journey results in **Intense Struggle** coupled with **Immense Suffering.** This is the most crucial period, termed by many

---

42   Kailash: The most sacred mountain peak in the Himalayas. This is considered to be the heavenly abode of Lord Shiva.

aspirants as the darkest hour of spirituality, and it has the most potential for trials and tribulations, with repeated failures and disappointments. For some, it may even lead to the abandonment of the whole pursuit.

"If one still persists against all odds, the day finally arrives where the **Inner Awakening** leads to **Illumination**. This is the story of the journey of inner transformation represented by the initial letter 'I' for each step. This signifies the evolution of the little "I" in ignorance to the super "I" in Illumination, and the other modifications of 'I' in between."

Vivek asked, "Chidanandji, so how do these steps relate to finding the peace within through the space between thoughts?"

"I am glad you asked this question. Bliss happens only when the mind is at rest. Think about it, when you sleep, your mind is at rest. It's not consumed with fulfilling worldly desires. And you wake up refreshed because your mind has been resting and not working overtime.

"When you question or think, because questioning is also a thought, your focus is away from your true self. And the sixty-five thousand thoughts you have a day are repeats from yesterday and are always focused on the past or future, which don't matter. Only the present moment matters. And even then, the present moment has no relevance because it instantly becomes the past. 'The present moment' implies a timeline, as though there were something before and something after. Therefore, the present moment is a lie: It is also unreal, like thoughts. Eternal presence is more important.

"It's interesting that we place more importance on our wakeful state than our dream state. When we are awake, thoughts appear and disappear in milliseconds. When we are in deep sleep, there are no thoughts, no memory, and no reasoning, only peace and bliss.

"Objects do not exist outside thought. For instance, you have data on memory cards and unless you plug them into a computer, you can't see them. Thoughts need the horsepower of your mind to experience them.

"Humans hunt after objects of pleasure for our immediate gratification. But the moment we understand that happiness is within us and not outside us, the objects aren't important anymore. Happiness occurs when we no longer desire anything.

"Thoughts are your objects of desire. The moment you focus on the space *between* your thoughts, you will automatically shift from the perpetual cycle of unhappiness to bliss. Just like music—it's not so much how the notes are played as the pauses between the notes that create the art of music. The same goes for the human mind.

"So, in essence, there is no difference between deep sleep and the space between your thoughts."

Chidanandji abruptly got up and everyone dispersed for lunch. But Vivek was too excited to rest after lunch. He kept mulling over Chidanandji's words. "What is this space between thoughts? How do I get there?" he wondered. He was so tangled up in his thoughts that he forgot about trying to find the space between them.

Chapter 15

Vivek was lost in his thoughts and the search for the space between his thoughts. When he tried to observe his thoughts, he hoped that he could locate the space where one thought ended and another one began. But the moment he noticed his first thought, he was already thinking the next thought and the cycle continued.

He was determined to continue. He knew he had to succeed in this exercise to become eligible to go the Bhageeratha Ghufa that Chidanandji had promised to take him to. He felt so near, yet so far. It was frustrating, to say the least. He tried to chant God's name, but except for some temporary peace of mind, it did not seem to help. He tried to meditate and fell into a state of drowsiness, half awake and half asleep. His back was hurting with all the meditative sitting every day for the past several days. His legs were cramping and his thoughts led to food because he was hungry, which became another thought altogether.

He kept dozing and waking up—perhaps hundreds of times. He would slip into oblivion and then suddenly wake up with a jolt. His frustration grew. Finally he felt heaviness in his body and felt as if his body were slipping away from him. He could feel electric vibrations moving with dizzying speed all over his body. He automatically focused on the spot between his eyebrows and felt a quivering sensation begin to emanate from there. It felt good. Waves of energy passed through different centers of his body and he could perceive them all converging in that space between his eyebrows.

He could literally see normally-invisible beings or ghostly figures, as well as scenery and the tiny, detailed, fine textures around him. Was he going into the body and observing the veins and the nerves and the cellular structure within, or was he expanding and floating in space, seeing the stellar spectacle of planets, stars and galaxies? Vivek had no idea, since he could not tell the difference. He was not aware of time and space. The only thing he was aware of was his existence, a transparent ghostly presence in a fuzzy universe that surrounded him.

And then it happened. He could actually observe a bunch of thoughts entering his mind just like a swarm of bees, a bundle of ropes or a bunch of snakes. He could then separate them string by string. He could stand apart and gaze at a single thought or what seemed like a single thought. But it was actually a conglomerate of several micro thoughts. There were thoughts within thoughts just like there is matter within space, space within matter and space within space. Was that the gap? He was not sure, but it certainly felt great. He felt a wave of bliss, a nothingness and carefreeness that he had never experienced before. Anything he thought became a vibrant presence.

He thought of Chidananda and there was the live image of Chidanandji. He could literally gaze into his sparkling eyes and see his white eyebrows, his sharp nose, his clean white teeth. Vivek was startled; the vision disappeared and the scenery changed. He was flying at low speed, which gradually increased to a higher speed as he cruised a few inches above sand dunes, roads, and forests. He could clearly see each pebble on the sand. He could smell each flower; he could feel the caress of each leaf. He was not just observing them. He was not just feeling them. He was living with them. He could zoom in and zoom out with amazing accuracy and control matter, space, thoughts, and feelings at any level. He felt as if he was in them, around them, over them and below them.

"Is this oneness? Is this Advaitha? Who knows?" he thought. But it certainly beat every experience he had ever had. He was no longer limited by his flesh, his cravings, his habits, his hang-ups. He wanted to cry, "I am free! I am free!" He wanted to float in this space of emptiness, absolutely unfettered and unlimited. He asked, "Where is my ego? Where has it gone?" An inner conviction answered back, "You were never your ego. It was a hallucination. It was a temporary imagining. There was no ego. There is no ego and there will never be any ego. There is only God. 'EGO' from now onward will mean to you 'Ever God's Oneness."

He was afraid to come back to normalcy. He was afraid to re-embrace his old tendencies. He wanted to stay in the state of peace and bliss forever. But it was not to be. A gentle touch on his forehead brought him back to this physical world. Chidanandji was standing over him. Chidanandji looked larger than life. He looked so magnificent, transcendent in his attire, a simple ochre-colored robe. Chidanandji looked like a resplendent flame.

Chidanandji whispered, "Vivek, wake up. You have been lost in samadhi[43] for over ten hours. It is now nine p.m. Get up very slowly lest you stumble. Drink this hot bowl of milk. The time has come to go to Bhageeratha Ghufa. You are now ready."

It took several minutes for Vivek to gather himself and shake away the vestiges of peace and bliss. He slowly got up, holding onto Chidanandji's extended hand, and then drank the hot milk in the bowl. Chidanandji led him outside the hut. The waning moon was playing hide-and-seek behind some clouds. Other than that, it was a clear night. As far as the eye could see, the stars shone brilliantly in night sky. It was like nowhere else in the world. A gentle breeze rustled through the valley, adding to the chill in the Himalayan air.

Vivek was humbled by his experience. "Chidanandji, what happened to me? Are we really going to Bhageeratha Ghufa? Am I really ready? Am I that lucky? I cannot believe it. You said I was in samadhi? Is this it? Do I still have a long way ahead?"

"Yes, you now have had a taste of samadhi. This is just the beginning," Chidanandji replied. "There is still a long road ahead of you. But you have been given a taste of the inner peace that's possible as you transcend into the space between your thoughts. But remember, though," he warned, "this experience is temporary. You go into a deep sleep every night, but when you wake up, you are the same person you were the previous day, with all your shortcomings and weaknesses. Initial stages in samadhi are also quite like this. However, you will retain a strong memory of the peace experienced during samadhi. What you have experienced is Savikalpa

---

[43] Samadhi: A state of total equanimity and priceless peace and bliss.

Samadhi, in which your mind was in perfect harmony with your chosen ideal as a form or a concept or a feeling.

"But from now on, you should be extremely careful. As you progress, you will be rewarded with God-given gifts and talents. Your intellect will become sharper. Your mind will be extremely alert. You will become broad-minded. But your ego will still be the same as it was before, and this is the real danger. Until the ego is destroyed, nothing has been accomplished. In many cases people develop pride for their trivial accomplishments and powers and become misguided souls who have fallen from spiritual grace."

"Chidanandji," Vivek said, "You helped me to experience this and because of that, I am eternally thankful."

Chidanandji placed a hand on Vivek's shoulder. "I didn't do this—you did. Your intense desire to experience the space between thoughts manifested in the experience you had. It's always within you. This was all part of the Divine plan to prepare you for the next stage of your journey with me."

Vivek was curious. "What's so special about Bhageeratha Ghufa, and why is this experience such a rarity?" He couldn't imagine, with all of the world's advanced technologies and GPS satellite systems, that there could even be an undiscovered inch of ground on the planet.

Chidanandji explained. "Generally after physical death, a person resides in the prana form for quite some time, which can range from a few earthly days to years, depending on how much he or she was attached to the world. The person transitions on to his or her mental or astral form and eventually into the causal form, until it is time to be born again either as a human or an animal or some other being to continue his progress toward perfection.

"Actually, you do transition back and forth from the physical to the astral to the causal form every day. When you're awake, you experience your physical form. When you dream, you experience your astral form. In deep sleep, you experience your causal form. Hence death and the phenomenon of other planes of existence are not new to a human being, though we all seem to be ignorant of that. Sleep is like death, and waking up is like birth. Getting a new physical body is like changing one's dress. Yet every one in the world is mortally afraid of death.

"Having said that, the ability to travel to these higher regions in the physical form and the ability to be simultaneously conscious of it are very rare for humans and only occur as a result of special blessings from God. Also the Bhageeratha cave belongs neither to the material realm nor to the astral region—it's a transmigratory world of its own. It is much finer than the physical cosmos but not as subtle as the astral cosmos. We will enter the Bhageeratha Ghufa by entering the icy current of the Ganga at Gomukh. In an instant, our material bodies will dematerialize and we will find ourselves in a new pranic form, looking almost the same as we do now, but much more vibrant, energetic, and, shall I say, beautiful and resplendent."

Vivek's excitement mingled with his trepidation. "That means that I'm going to die as this physical form?"

"The answer is yes and no," Chidanandji continued, "You will die as the physical body, but your connection with the world is not severed. You will spend your time with me in the higher planes of existence for however long you are supposed to be there. When you return to earth—and believe me, you will return to earth—you will enter a new body that will look and feel exactly like the body you have now. However, your inner being will be totally recharged and made fresh by your divine experience and exuberance. Are you familiar with the game of cricket[44]?

"Somewhat, though I never played it." Vivek replied.

"When a batsman hits a cricket ball out of the grounds, they generally replace it with another ball, a new ball which has been handled and massaged to be as close as possible in age (in terms of the number of times it was bowled by the bowler) to the ball that was hit out," Chidanandji went on. "In a similar manner, your brand-new body will look and behave like the older body you left behind. In that sense this experience is like death, because your old physical body dematerializes completely. However, it is unlike death, because you return to the almost-same body to live

---

[44]   Cricket: A game played in India and many colonial countries. It is very similar to baseball, but is a game dominated by the hitter, who is called the batsman. The pitcher is called a bowler. Unlike a baseball game, which has low scores, cricket is a high-scoring game and is played not just for hours but for days at a time.

under the same conditions in the identical environment you left behind." Chidanandji noted Vivek's confused expression. "If you find it hard to digest this concept, consider this. This body that you sport is not literally the same body that you had when you were five year old, in terms of the size, shape and the cells inside the body. Or even the same one you had yesterday or this morning because your cells have already changed. They're constantly changing. The only thing that is the same is your spirit residing in your physical body."

"I get the idea," Vivek said. "But it's still unnerving to think that I will be leaving my body behind to dematerialize."

"Now you understand why it is a rare phenomenon and a rare privilege," Chidanandji said. "However, I am not privy to the reason why you were chosen for this experience and not Amanda. If you remember, in her previous birth, when she was Saraswathi, our spiritual master forbade her to focus on the space between her thoughts. Since she did not listen, she had to undergo another birth to work out her karma. In your case, you are encouraged. Why? God only knows. Let us now go back into the hut. But I am going to ask you once more whether you really want to go through this experience. You are perfectly free to choose either way. You can walk away from me and this experience. I won't feel disappointed. I will ask someone to take you back to Rishikesh and Hardiwar and go with you to Delhi and put you on a plane to America. Or, if you so desire, I can instantly teleport you to your penthouse in Manhattan. Of course, I need to remember to stamp your passport so that everything looks in order. Tell me, what do you want?"

Vivek was shivering and shuddering when he heard this. He felt knots growing in his stomach, as well as butterflies fluttering around. He was trying to respond when Chidanandji came near and whispered in his ear, "You do not have to decide now. If you want to come, meet me at the hot springs at three a.m. tomorrow morning. Have a good night's sleep." He walked out of the hut and soon disappeared in the darkness.

Vivek sat pensively on top of his sleeping bag. It was all too much for him to grasp. He tried to sleep but was too excited to relax. He could not tell whether he was overjoyed or excessively fearful. He thought Chidanandji would come back to the hut to sleep, but he didn't. He lay awake thinking about his body dematerializing and eventually materialized into a deep sleep.

Chapter 16

Vivek woke up and looked at his Rolex watch. It was 2:45 a.m. Except for his watch, he had no other electronics that were working due to the intense cold of the Himalayan Mountains. He knew what he wanted to do and had come too far to turn back. It was time to take the plunge. He got up and quickly rolled up his sleeping bag. He put on his heaviest sweater and socks, slipped into his hiking shoes and ventured into the darkness towards the hot springs.

The entire village was asleep. He could hear the crickets in the distant forest and the gentle murmur of the animals as he made his way through the dark to the hot springs. He shed his clothes in the bone-chilling cold and stepped into the warm water. As he bathed in the warmth of the spring, he was greeted by the stately figure of Chidanandji sitting on a raised platform next to it. Chidanandji said gently, "I knew you would come." He motioned for Vivek to approach him and handed him a bundle of clothes.

"Vivek," he said, "Where we are going, there is no need for your Western dress. You can wear this robe and you'll be fine. After you take a bath in the hot springs, apply this herbal oil to your body. Also eat these balls of herbal mixture that I have collected over the last several days from inaccessible places in the Himalayan slopes. This plant is a distant cousin of the legendary somalata[45] plant and will rejuvenate you so that you will not require food,

---

[45] Somalata: A legendary plant that grows in the heights of the Himalayan Mountains, well known for its potency for longevity of life and rejuvenation of the physical body.

rest, or sleep for the next several weeks. Leave your clothes and shoes in the hut and wear these wooden sandals. Also leave your backpack behind. Hurry up. We do not have a lot of time."

Vivek quietly accepted the bundle of clothes and proceeded to the hut. He was ready in a few minutes. In his new attire, he looked like a clone of Chidanandji in his lightweight clothing and sandals. Oddly, after eating the herbs, Vivek did not feel the Himalayan cold at all. It was as if he were in sunny Hawaii. He met up with Chidanandji and they quickly walked down the slopes and proceeded towards Gomukh. Chidanandji walked like a man possessed, unmindful of the bushes and the stony slopes. By the time they arrived at the icy entrance of the Gomukh and approached the boulders between which the Ganga emerged in her fury, the first rays of the morning sun had started streaming across the sky between the mountain peaks. Chidanandji held Vivek's hand and whispered, "Do not be afraid, no matter what happens. Hold tightly onto my hand. Do exactly as I tell you. Focus your attention between your eyebrows and on the space between your thoughts. Follow me."

Holding Chidanandji's hand, Vivek slowly stepped into the rushing gorge. Fear struck him, but he held on tightly to Chidanandji's hand. He thought they would freeze to death, though he felt neither the cold nor the swift currents of the gorge. They waded slowly and steadily through the waters along the banks, nearing the entrance of the cave. As they waded into deep water, suddenly they were swept off their feet, and they both started to drown. Vivek could feel his body being tossed around, thrown apart, but he did not let go of Chidanandji's hand. He could hear the gentle whisper of Chidanandji saying, "Why fear when I am here?"

Vivek could witness every part, cell, and sinew of his body being ripped apart and churned around. Both Chidanandji and Vivek were in a state of quiescence for what seemed like a long time. Vivek had no idea how long it was. Finally they both emerged from the icy waters inside a huge cavern.

The cavern was so big that it appeared to be a land within a land, a garden in the bowels of the mountains. It was spectacular. Behind him, he could see the narrow mouth of the Gomukh entrance, through which the sun's rays were peeping in. He also saw the Ganges flowing in her majesty and fury. While the outside was full of snow and icy cold, the inside of the cavern resembled a heavenly garden, at once tropical and Mediterranean. Flowering plants, fruit trees, butterflies, and birds abounded. The entire place was filled with the aroma of jasmine, rose, and every flower one could imagine.

He looked around and saw Chidanandji gently stepping out of the water. "Oh, my God," thought Vivek. Chidanandji truly looked like a god. He looked a good deal younger and more energetic. His clothes were shining and colorful. His skin was glowing. Vivek looked at himself and he could not believe what he saw: He also looked resplendent. They both exuded heavenly beauty. They did not have to talk to each other. Vivek was able to read Chidanandji's thoughts and vice versa. From that point on, they conversed through their thoughts.

Chidanandji saw the excitement in Vivek's eyes. He motioned him to stay silent and guided him slowly through the beautiful floral path along the banks of the gushing river. This place looked like the Garden of Eden, like the Shangri-la or the Swarga[46] that is described in the scriptures of the various religions. The melodious music of the many birds filled the air. Vivek thought he also heard divine flute music in the distance and Vedic chanting coming from far off. The whole place was a lush green, a total contrast to what they had seen outside Gomukh. The ceiling of the cavern was so high—perhaps a thousand feet high—and it felt as if God had created a natural biosphere inside the mountain. They had hardly walked a quarter mile when Vivek was startled to see the most glorious sight he had ever witnessed in his life. He was breathless for a few seconds, as he could not believe what he saw.

The cavern suddenly opened and became much larger, with a central dome-like structure that rose to perhaps two thousand feet or more. He could see the bright rays of the sun falling through the giant uppermost window in the cavern, which was as wide as several football fields. What was even more impressive was the enormous amount of water that gushed forth from the top of the cavern in a torrential flow, caressing the sides of the cavern walls to fall down onto a massive ellipsoidal rock which itself was several hundred feet high and a thousand feet wide. The force of the

---

[46] Swarga: Sanskrit word for Heaven.

waterfall was so great and the volume of the water so extensive that it made a deafening roar and generated a cloud mist of water droplets that extended thousands of feet around the waterfall.

Chidanandji came near and whispered, "This is Aakaasa Ganga[47] as it was millennia ago. What you perceive as the massive rock which receives the waterfall was Lord Shiva Himself, who took the massive torrent on the locks of his hair to slow down the mighty force of the Ganga. He later transformed himself into an ovoid stone (Shivalinga). This is the most revered and holy spot in this area. Anyone who spends even a fraction of a second in this vicinity is transported into transcendental bliss. There is a statue of sage Bhageeratha (who was instrumental for the sacred descent of the Ganga) inside the garden adjacent to the waterfalls. I will take you there."

Vivek noticed that Chidanandji was much more agile, strong, and sprightly than he had been at Tapovan. He seemed to glide on the road, which was paved with polished rocks of brilliant colors. They prayed to the statue of Bhageeratha and then sat on a bench.

Vivek picked up Chidanandji's thoughts. "Vivek, I need to give you a very clear idea about the Bhageeratha cave and the spiritual beings that you will encounter here. First of all, you and I are in our transmigratory bodies, which are neither physical nor astral. This is a temporary form given to us to freely roam around the heavens and the higher planes of existence. Your physical form of Vivek as you know it has gone back to its elements, but as I mentioned, a brand-new physical form of Vivek will be created for you when the Divine decides to return us to earth and to our ways of living. In earthly terms, it is as if we have come on temporary visitor visas, compared to others who have come on business visas, family visas, etcetera. As long as you are with me, we will be granted permission to visit all the lokas [48], or planes of existence."

---

[47]   Aakaasa : Sky.

[48]   Lokas: The various planes of existence, such as physical, astral and causal. It is believed that there are 14 such planes of consciousness. Man's physical existence is right in the middle.

"Here everything is made of mental stuff, even though it looks as real and tangible as the physical universe. Here people do not eat to live, they eat for the pleasure of eating. Also here people do not enjoy the senses on account of being slaves to their desires or on account of compulsion. They have the freedom to enjoy everything so long as they do not interfere with others' freedom. There are no police, military, or warriors here. Everything is based on self-governance. Unlike the earth people, the beings here do not toil or need to work hard to accomplish anything.

"Whenever they need anything, they just have to wish or think about and it will instantly appear before them. When I say anything, I mean anything: knowledge, wisdom, fine arts, music, talents, you name it. Nothing is beyond their reach. The only thing that eludes them here is the highest stage of realization of desirelessness. I must also add, though, that if they want to meet the highest masters and avatars in this plane then they need to pray very humbly. For the final realization, however, the beings here have to be reborn on earth to live a life of austerity, sacrifice, prayer, and service."

"Here people have no regrets, no complaints, since everything is abundant in measure, and there is no paucity of anything. Almost all of the people are very affectionate and friendly beings. Also, since everyone's thoughts and feelings are transparent to everyone else, they behave very carefully and follow a heavenly decorum of behavior.

"Rarely will you find souls here who are upset, angry, jealous, or greedy. Usually new souls who have just arrived here from earth are trying to adapt and may be a bit depressed, angry, or resentful. But that quickly fades. Though there is tremendous freedom, there is tremendous discipline also. Everyone here is supposed to know their jurisdiction of powers and is expected to operate within those boundaries.

"Generally people do not gossip here or assemble in large crowds. They either tend to be alone or in small groups of extremely like-minded people. They have all arrived at this place with a specific plan to enjoy certain experiences. All beings here are also in some sense temporary residents. After their stay is over, which is decided by their own desires, they go back to earth or to any other plane of existence as appropriate in the grand scheme of things and the roles that they are expected to play.

"This place is the source of all ideas, philosophical thoughts, musical masterpieces, and treasures of arts and cultures. Those whom you call geniuses and inventors and great thinkers on earth are those who are able to connect to these inspirations in a moment of egolessness. Everyone tries to live their lives as naturally as possible without any pretensions whatsoever."

"Wow!" thought Vivek. "This is heaven on earth!"

"That's right," Chidanandji agreed.

"So then, why would anyone want to leave this beautiful place?" Vivek asked.

"I will not answer that question now," Chidanandji said. "I do not want to prejudice you. You will see the people yourself. You may even converse with them. You may learn from them. You may even meet the highest masters of great fame and earthly renown."

Vivek couldn't believe what he was hearing. "You mean I could meet someone like Jesus, Buddha, Rama, or Krishna?"

"Absolutely, if that is what you truly want," Chidanandji replied. "However, for that to happen, you need go to the Garden of the Wish-Fulfilling Tree. We will go there sometime in the future. By the way, there is no sunrise or sunset here. You will never get tired and you will never go to sleep. You never need to eat unless you desire to taste food for the sake of taste."

"So there is no disease or death here," Vivek observed. Chidanandji nodded. "That means that there is only pleasure and fun and no worries and challenges. Am I right?" Vivek asked. Chidanandji nodded again.

Vivek came to a realization. "Wait a minute. If I have no problems to face, or can't help anyone because no one needs help, and I can simply have fun all of the time, it must get boring. If everyone is doing their own thing, they don't need the affection of others. And if they don't need that, they don't need love from others, either."

"Vivek, you are a fast learner," Chidanandji said. "There is love here, which is more on the nature of politeness and amicability. It's not that emotional, tear-filled feeling of intensity and affection that we call love on earth."

"But," Vivek began, "if there is no love, then this is not heaven; this must be hell."

"Believe me, this is heaven," Chidanandji reassured him. "This is what your religions have promised you if you lead a righteous life. But we do have a valley here that we call the forbidden zone, and which you may think of as hell."

"Why?" Vivek was taken aback by Chidanandji's statement. How could hell coexist with heaven?

Chidanandji explained, "Some spirits, due to their strong earthly attachments, turn unruly and denounce the laws and cause uneasiness in the other residents here in heaven. Such beings are caught and dispatched to the forbidden valley, where we have simulated earth-like conditions in which they suffer like slaves. Everyone is forced to do the things that they hate to do most. There they toil for a long time or as much time as needed to get a feeling for the consequences of their own actions. They generally come to understand fairly quickly the chain-reaction of consequences that is karma."

"Is that where they learn the effect of their behavior on others?" Vivek asked.

"Yes, but in hell, they are learning under pressure, under strict supervision and not of their own volition. Such learning does not last long," Chidanandji replied.

"In that case, Chidanandji, I think that earth is a much better place than both heaven and hell," Vivek said. "In heaven you keep on enjoying without learning anything. In hell you learn under compulsion. On earth you have the freedom to learn or not to learn, to help or to sin, to love or to hate, to heal or to hurt. I love the earthly existence. I don't want either heaven or hell. True love is possible only on earth. Now I understand why the spirits want to leave heaven and hell after some time and want to return back to earth, and why true realization is possible only on earth. This has been a fascinating revelation to me. All along I thought one goes to heaven just like one goes into retirement."

Chidanandji smiled. "Vivek, you really are an amazingly fast learner. Now I know why I was instructed to bring you here. You have the built-in renunciation to see through things. You were not fascinated by heaven. I myself did not feel or think like you when I came here for the first time at almost the same age as you are now. But come, let us take this trail and see what happens."

Chapter 17

As Chidanandji and Vivek walked along the trail, Vivek was amazed by everything he saw. So far it felt as if they were the only ones in the Bhageeratha cave. Suddenly, a ways off, he saw the beings of that region for the first time. A man and woman were walking majestically towards them a few hundred feet away. Vivek saw that they were both very tall, the man standing at about seven feet and the woman only a few inches shorter. Both were exquisitely beautiful, with golden complexions and very sharp features. Everything about them was graceful—the way they walked, their mannerisms, their body language.

Engrossed in their conversation, neither the man nor the woman noticed Chidanandji or Vivek at first. But Vivek was mesmerized by their enthralling presence. They wore resplendent robes, and there was a bright aura around them. At the last second, the woman noticed Chidanandji. She walked up, greeted him and touched his feet in a gesture of respect. The man followed suit. The penetrating eyes of the woman fell on Vivek. He was transported into realms of great joy seeing such ethereal beauty. She did not say a word, but smiled, and the handsome couple walked away.

Vivek turned to Chidanandji. "Who are these heavenly beings? They seem to know you."

Chidanandji smiled. "These are kindred spirits of a very high order of what you may consider as angels. They are God's deputies and help anyone and everyone assigned to them. It seems as if they are in between assignments and are enjoying their peace. They love to discuss Advaitha philosophy and have spent countless hours with me on the earth plane."

Vivek could hardly contain his excitement. Angels! He had actually witnessed the presence of angels, the most benevolent of beings celebrated throughout the centuries! But something nagged within and he was at first embarrassed to ask Chidanandji the next question.

Chidanandji sensed his unease and said, "I know that you are wondering why you still had human emotions such as attraction when you first saw the angelic woman. Don't worry, Vivek. That is only natural. As I mentioned earlier, you and I are not in the astral form, but in the transmigratory form, which is a mixture of the physical and the astral. Hence, you still retain many human qualities such as guilt, lust, and resentment. Don't think that just because you are experiencing this that you instantly shed your mental state from the physical world. You have to be on your guard all the time especially after experiencing inner peace, otherwise you will easily slip back into your old ways. Practice and detachment are essential for your success in the spiritual realm. Do not worry too much about such distractions and feelings. These thoughts don't really belong to you—they are only passing clouds. Only if you pay too much attention to them will they harm you by clinging to you. If you ignore them, they will go away. Do not let these linger long enough to become part of your psyche and harden into habits that cannot be easily conquered.

"By the way," he went on. "What would you like to see here? I can take you to the various centers of excellence where beings excel in music, arts, science, philosophy, and ultimately to the Garden of the Wish-Fulfilling Tree. Tell me, what do you want to see next and in what sequence?"

Vivek's excitement grew again. "Chidanandji, I would love to take in everything, but would like you to choose, if you don't mind. I'm so excited that I can't make up my mind."

"Sure." Chidanandji nodded. "I understand. How about we visit the Hall of Science first? I know that you are fascinated by science and technology." With that, they started their trek towards their first destination.

After awhile, they entered a futuristic-looking building. Vivek gazed around him and felt as though he had entered the pages of a science-fiction novel. All kinds of gadgets, devices, computers, and thought machines were on display and hundreds of men and women were deeply engrossed in a multitude of scientific experiments. Chidanandji explained, "This entire region is called the Hiranya Garba—the golden egg. This is the source of all ideas that manifest on earth and other planes of consciousness. The beings you see are what you refer to as scientists, engineers, and professionals on the earth plane who were constantly engaged in unraveling the secrets of nature during their physical lifetimes. There is an angelic spirit who leads this effort and you can ask him about what goes on here."

The moment Chidanandji uttered these words, a person who almost looked like Einstein, with disheveled white hair and sharp eyes, wearing a meticulous white suit, glided in front of them. He greeted Chidanandji with great affection and introduced himself to Vivek as Arametheus.

Arametheus said to them, "Welcome, earthly spirits. I am so happy to see you here. I can tell that you are unlike other beings who have come here after their physical death to spend time on their favorite innovations, the ones they could not complete on the earth plane. To me, it seems as if you are distinguished visitors on a temporary visit of great importance. It also seems as though this young man is greatly interested in what we are doing here. Please ask me anything. I'm happy to provide the answers."

"Sir Arametheus," Vivek said, "It's a great pleasure to meet you. I've always been fascinated by technology. I would like to know what kinds of inventions and futuristic research are being conducted here."

Arametheus nodded. "This is the where the brightest and most brilliant minds and intellects come together. Here, you will see Aristotle working hand in hand with Einstein. You will also see Archimedes explaining his experiences to Darwin.

"The emphasis here is on knowledge for the sake of knowledge and for the ultimate good of created beings, not just human beings on earth but in other regions in the universe as well. Here, we know for a fact that the body dies, but thoughts persist much longer than the physical body, just as the earth may exist for a billion years while a human lives only for a hundred years. Thoughts last longer than the physical universe, and yet they are also unreal and transitory compared to the consciousness. This place is the source and repository of all thoughts during one cycle of creation, which may span billions of earth years. We are mental beings and whatever we think here instantly happens. In that sense all scientific experiments and discoveries in this place are just thought experiments. Yet they are more real than any scientific experiment on the earth plane.

"The people in your world are limited in their understanding. The scientists there believe that everything is physical. They refuse to believe that there is a mental or astral universe which is more vast than the physical universe, or that there is an even bigger universe of consciousness which is still more vast than the astral universe."

He went on, "There has been tremendous progress in physics, chemistry, biology, and the engineering and material sciences, as well as in medicine. Yet most scientific discoveries and innovations are being used either to make money or to control others through misused military power.

"Modern physics talks about the vastness of the physical cosmos, as well as the grandeur of the microcosm or the universe of electrons and fundamental particles. It is as if man can never find the extremes—the larger than the largest or the smaller than the smallest. This seems to be a never-ending search."

Vivek listened intently. What this angelic being was saying struck him as profoundly true. Arametheus paused briefly to let Vivek absorb what he'd said before continuing. "Humans are also faced with so many riddles. They have discovered galaxies and supernovas millions of light years away. They talk about black holes and worm holes. Matter mysteriously disappears as if evaporated into thin air or sucked into a black hole, only to suddenly appear somewhere else. Humans talk about the uncertain behavior of electrons, as well as of matter and anti-matter, and about how time and space are interrelated and how one cannot exist without the other. How about the fundamental limit on the speed of light? Why is it one hundred eighty-six thousand miles per second? Or is the speed of light really a fundamental limit? What are the constituents of quarks? What are the basic units of string theory, the so-called strings? Are they real or figments of one's imagination?

"Scientists say everything started with the Big Bang and that since then, the universe has been expanding with ever-increasing speed. But what was before the Big Bang? And when, how, and why did it originate? Is there a creator, and, if so, where is this creator? Is all of this random phenomena? What is the relationship between mind and matter? Or does it matter? Humans are constantly tangled in the labyrinth of their thoughts with these questions.

"These questions will remain as riddles as long as humans believe only in their physical existence and refuse to connect the mental to the physical universe. Once you accept the basic premise that you are not just your physical body, but rather five layers of systems—the body, breath, mind (which corresponds to thought), intellect (for discriminating among pieces of information), and heart (for feelings), everything will fit into place. Science is not willing to accept this model, since human physical instruments cannot measure phenomena in other dimensions or spaces.

"Believing that everything is physical, scientists posit theories about the origins of the universe, and try to explain phenomena such as black holes. Everything that is created has to eventually die or change state. What happens in a black hole is that the physical material disappears and transforms into the astral world. When a vast galaxy or star dies, its massive bulk converts into a small black hole where its energy is sucked into the astral world with a tremendous force.

"The speed of light is a constant only in the physical universe and is governed by the laws of physics and its limitations. However, at atomic scales, the fundamental particles can and do exceed the speed of light. If the universe keeps on expanding at an increasingly faster rate, eventually the periphery of the universe will travel faster than light. In the higher planes of existence, one travels at the speed of thought, which is almost instantaneous. Traveling physically to a distant galaxy may take several thousands of light years. But that's only in the realm of the physical body. Since your thoughts exist in the astral realm, you can instantly travel in the mind to a distant planet. Though this is not demonstrable on the earth plane, this is the modus operandi in the astral plane, even in this semi-physical astral plane." Arametheus motioned to the activities around him. "Scientists can never find the answers to all of their questions about creation by investigating the physical plane alone. As a matter of fact, the nature of consciousness cannot be understood in any of the planes of existence unless one is willing and able to transcend all of them."

A thought then occurred to Vivek. "Sir Arametheus, if beings here in this heavenly sphere are more intelligent and operate on mental powers, it seems as if they already know many things far beyond the comprehension of the ordinary human mind. What could they possibly be interested in discovering if there is no money to be gained from it?"

Arametheus answered, "There is no concept of money here as on the earth plane. Everything is free and in abundance and hence there is no competition or control or intellectual arrogance as there is on earth. We are trying to simply bridge the gap between science and spirituality. We still work on many things, such as medical advances, a fundamental understanding of the nature of the human race, better political and governance systems, and ultimately the cause of creation. The last question has eluded answers almost forever, but we do not give up. Though we believe we can answer all questions through rational thinking, we do understand the limitations of our mind and intellect.

"As far as medical research is concerned, we know that physicians on earth focus more on symptoms than on cures. The reason is that if there are no patients, there is no money for the medical industry. But what they don't understand is that thoughts and feelings are the true source of disease. Hence, the cure is found within our own minds and feelings. Modern medicine can only help to alleviate suffering and pain at the physical level. The ultimate medicine is the most potent of all forces, namely love itself. Have I answered some of your questions, Vivek?" Arametheus asked.

Vivek nodded. "More than I can handle in one discussion, it seems. I've learned more in our discussion than I would have learned in a lifetime on earth. Thank you so much for your wisdom and insight."

Chidanandji, who had been quiet in contemplation, then spoke up. "It's nice to see a rational thinking scientist open up to the power of love. I know these discussions could go on endlessly, but I think that it's time that Vivek talk to someone about the advances in music and the fine arts, too. Thank you, my friend, for the gift of your thoughts and love."

The moment Chidanandji mentioned this, an exquisitely dressed, beautiful woman with a charming smile started walking towards them. Arametheus turned as she walked up and introduced herself as Zwela, the angelic being overseeing all artistic and musical activities. Zwela greeted both Chidanandji and Vivek with great affection.

"I will take over from here, Arametheus," she said. "Let me introduce you to our center of excellence in the fine arts, and if you wish, you can accompany me to see a multitude of artists enraptured in music, dance and art. We pursue these talents as the natural extension of our expressions towards perfection. For instance, music and spiritually are closely intertwined. We focus more on the subtle aspects of music, like melody, rather than on the harsh noise that some humans on earth refer to as music. When we sing a tune in a particular melody here, for instance, we immediately witness the effect, like a lamp lighting up.

"Music, dance, and painting are natural expressions of the heart and must be soulful. They reflect the personality and feelings of the creator of the art and can be enjoyed only by those with a similar understanding and capability. We compose music that can heal and calm the mind and create feelings of love and devotion.

"We've learned the painful consequences of using the fine arts on earth to promote violence and abuse of other human beings on earth. Those among us who still insist on using the fine arts to that end are sent to the forbidden valley that you call hell.

"Come, I shall take you to the Great Hall of the Arts." She motioned for Chidanandji and Vivek to follow her. She led them out of the Hall of Science and through exquisite gardens of the most beautiful trees, plants, and flowers that Vivek had ever seen, as the swirl of sounds emanating from the humming bees and singing birds rose up around them. Vivek felt as though he were a note on a musical scale, playing in a symphony of sounds as he glided towards the great hall, which appeared to vibrate with intense energy from a distance.

Once inside, he was in awe of the great works of art surrounding him as he glided down majestic halls—the *Mona Lisa* appeared to smile at him as he moved past her, the marble figure of David also seemed to acknowledge his presence as he sat in his ageless contemplative state, a testament of Michelangelo's genius. He even thought that he caught a glimpse of Monet talking to Picasso as the two creative intellects paired up to add elements of perspective and light to a painting of a world never seen before. As he continued down a hall of art that reflected the spirit of the Renaissance, with every masterpiece he passed, he felt enlightened and overjoyed. His passion for the arts resonated through every fiber of his astral being as he came to understand the insight, intuition, inspiration, and genius that sees beyond the limitations of the physical eye, and which senses the world from a different perspective, understanding how the parts fit into the whole, where harmony resonates, cutting out the din of chaos and confusion. From the mythical sculptures of ancient Greek gods to the renderings of scenes painted onto ancient Roman pottery, he could see that the arts had painted the tapestry of human civilization for as long as humans had roamed the earth.

Vivek was lulled into semi-consciousness by the melodic strains resonating throughout the great hall. He passed by a room where he saw Beethoven and Mozart jointly composing a new concerto. At last, they entered the Great Hall of Arts through a set of massive bronze paneled doors. The hall resembled the Florentine cathedral the Duomo, designed by the great Renaissance architect Brunelleschi in the fifteenth century.

Vivek gazed around him inside the giant domed hall and marveled at the scenes depicted on the stained glass windows and on the frescoes surrounding him on all sides. The vastness of the dome and its simplicity in art and architecture was its crowning achievement.

Chidanandji broke the silence of the setting by asking Zwela, "Why don't you sing for us? It has been a long time since I've heard you sing."

Zwela extended her hand and immediately a stringed instrument materialized in it. Vivek was now becoming used to these miraculous events and was enraptured not only by the beauty surrounding him, but also by the beauty of her voice when she began to sing and play the instrument. He could neither decipher the language nor recognize the tune. It seemed to be from an ancient language unknown to him. Regardless, her voice hypnotized him as he was lifted by the notes and transported to a state of indescribable peace, happiness, and bliss. When her song ended, her voice hung suspended in the air, as if the song had taken on a life of its own, reverberating throughout the great domed hall. Vivek didn't want it to end and could have stayed there forever, but knew that Chidanandji had other plans for him.

With visions of great architectural marvels, ancient sculptures, masterpieces of musical composition, and life-like Renaissance paintings imprinted in his memory, Vivek bade goodbye to the angelic being Zwela and continued on his journey with Chidanandji.

After a short time, they arrived at the hidden valley; the place of hell. Chidanandji came close to Vivek and murmured, "I have willed that we be invisible in this land. I cannot take the risk of you becoming a victim here."

Vivek looked around. It looked the same as the rest of the astral plane, only gloomier, lonelier, and darker. The beings around them were clearly not happy. Vivek was startled to realize that their expressions, body language, and violent thoughts were exactly like those of the people on earth, especially the ones bustling around large metropolitan areas. Most of them were running around doing something as if propelled by an insane invisible inner force. Some of them were clearly too tired to continue but were unable to put a stop to their work. Vivek couldn't help but think that he was observing inmates in a prison or insane asylum. Some were constantly running around, others talking to themselves and others toiling without any rest.

"Chidanandji," Vivek said. "These people are working endlessly and not enjoying anything. They're verbally and physically abusing each other and feeling pleasure from it. My goodness, this reminds me of earth!"

"That's because they're still attached to material things from earth or to feelings like hatred," Chidanandji explained. "Heaven and hell exist in the mind. Here they're consumed by their own worries, ambitions, thought patterns and desires. They can't run away from their thoughts until they choose to release them and go to heaven or reincarnate back to earth. In heaven, beings are able to detach themselves from their own mind to enjoy peace.

"I do not want to spend too much time here," he said. "I just wanted you to see what hell is like. Let us now go to the Garden of the Wish-Fulfilling Tree. A great wonder awaits you there."

Chapter 18

After what seemed like several hours, Chidanandji and Vivek arrived at a spacious garden which, like the first glimpse he'd had of the lush world inside the glacier, resembled Vivek's notion of the Garden of Eden. All kinds of flowers and trees, especially fig, which is the most sacred tree mentioned in all religious scriptures, grew abundantly there. At the center of the garden was a giant banyan tree, which seemed to spread over several acres. The canopy was supported by a multitude of branches with a web of roots at its base.

"This is the Wish-Fulfilling Tree," Chidanandji said. The two of them stood under the massive, entwining branches and Chidanandji advised Vivek to sit on the ground, close his eyes, and again focus on the area in between his eyebrows and on the space between his thoughts. He also directed him to clearly picture in his mind what he wanted to see.

Vivek followed Chidanandji's instructions and soon lost body consciousness. He clearly pictured what he wanted and whom he wanted to see. The next thing he noticed was that he was standing in a beautifully decorated and spacious outdoor amphitheater that held what looked to be thousands of seats. The place was filled with a divine aroma and gentle music played somewhere nearby.

Slowly he began to see a great number of beings entering and taking their seats—beings of different ages, cultures, and genders. Soon the amphitheater was packed as everyone eagerly waited for the arrival of the guests of honor. After what felt like at least an hour, the honored attendees arrived and took their seats on the stage.

Vivek couldn't believe who he was seeing: Gautam Buddha was seated on the left, and next to him was Jesus Christ. In the middle was Sri Krishna, flanked by Moses and the Prophet Mohammed. In the row below the stage were seated the founders of every religion and system of philosophy known to humankind. Vivek was surprised to see Chidanandji among them. He realized, for the first time, the degree of honor bestowed on Chidanandji in heaven.

Just then, a saintly person acting as the master of ceremonies got up and spoke through thought. In heaven, there was no language barrier.

"I salute the manifested Divinity in every one of you, my friends," he began. "Today is a very special day. We have among us the founders, prophets or avatars of five major religions, as well as the founders of every other minor religion or philosophical thought process from the past five thousand years of human history. We are also very blessed to welcome Gautam Buddha, Jesus Christ, Bhagavan Krishna, Moses, and the Prophet Mohammed. They have all come together to deliver a special message to all of us with the hope that this message will be eventually carried to earth.

"Though there are several planes of consciousness, as well as several civilizations similar to the human population on earth in the distant galaxies, we all know that the earth and its inhabitants hold a special place in our hearts. It is a widely acknowledged secret that the earth is the final portal prior to emancipation, freedom, or nirvana. I welcome all whole-heartedly and without further ado, I would like to invite our heavenly speakers, the jewels of our ancient wisdom, to speak to us."

Gautam Buddha rose majestically from his seat; he looked radiant and peaceful.

The Buddha spoke. "It has been quite awhile since I have given a speech. It is a great pleasure to be among my divine brethren—Jesus, Krishna, Moses, and Mohammed, and of course everyone else assembled here. I agreed to attend this meeting because of the urgency of the threat posed by religious fanaticism and national parochialism, which have resulted in so much violence and war.

"You all know that a religion called Buddhism, dedicated to my name, has a very large following on earth—except in its birthplace. As a matter of fact, I myself do not recognize most of the teachings and rituals attributed to me. Under no circumstances can I condone violence by those who are supposed to be devoted to the principle of nonviolence in thought, word, and deed.

"I really thought I had set a good example, but unfortunately my followers seemed not to have paid heed. When I was on earth, I gave a lecture a day for almost sixty or more years and taught my disciples numerous methods of meditation. Yet those teachings seem to have been wasted.

"I purposely did not preach the aspect of a personal God, since I saw that those who claimed to have devotion to a personal God and who followed the so-called rituals had done more harm than good. That is the reason why I taught the Sunya Vadha, the emptiness theory: so everyone could become nothing. Actually, the one who truly becomes nothing becomes everything—that was the secret of my teaching, but alas, no one seems to understand or care anymore.

"I urge all of you Buddhists and followers of other faiths to live in harmony. The founders of these religions who are seated here are in peace with one another based on mutual respect and total harmony. Please let it be known that we did not establish the religions; the religions were founded in our names after we left. Why do the followers posit all these differences and fight bloody wars to prove who is right and who is superior? Don't they see their own hypocrisy? Are they that blind not to see their own faults? I bless you all so that you can go within and bring out the source of love that is in abundance within you."

With those words, Gautam Buddha sat down and everyone cheered loudly. It was now time for Jesus to talk. With equal majesty, he came to the center of the podium and addressed the gathering. If Buddha exuded compassion, Jesus seemed to be the embodiment of love.

Jesus said, "I invoke the blessings of the Father in Heaven who is in each and every one of us. I am greatly honored to be here, along with the loving and compassionate beings on the stage. As a body, I was a humble carpenter. I personally do not feel I am in the same league as these Divine beings. However, as the spirit, I and my Father are one, and hence, I am the spirit in every one of you.

"I am saddened by the many acts that have been committed in my name. Granted, a few noble souls who were inspired by my teachings have done a great service to humanity, but much more evil and deception have been perpetrated in the name of religion. My teachings have been distorted so much that when I read the Bible, I recognize only portions of what I originally taught.

"The Christians and the Jews are awaiting the second coming, but honestly, if I were to return to earth as I am now, they would reject me and label me as the anti-Christ. It's ironic that they fear what they call Satan when the real Satan and evil reside in their thoughts and ego and manifest in anger, jealousy, greed, lust, and misery.

"I whole-heartedly support the plea of my elder brother Buddha for people of various religions to rise above their minds, egos, and judgments and start discovering the commonality of the human race that binds us together. The ego creates division and the spirit brings us together as one."

The gathered gave Jesus a standing ovation as he turned and bowed humbly to his fellow beings on the stage. Each one reverently acknowledged his grace and humility in return through mutual respect and understanding. Soon Moses got up to transmit his thoughts as the next speaker. His face shone brilliantly and he glowed as if bathed in light.

Said Moses, "I offer my greetings to everyone. I was enthralled by the words of my younger brother Jesus, as well as those of Gautam Buddha. I represent the Almighty Jehovah and the faith of the twelve tribes of Israel. In terms of chronological age, I am second only to my elder brother Krishna.

"All religions have a common source in the formless aspect of God. The Jews as a community have suffered enormously at the hands of other human beings in spite of their extraordinary devotion to Jehovah. Almost every religion on earth has warred with others over the centuries to dispute whose faith is superior and which people are closest to God's heart, while in truth we are all part of God. God is universal and equal towards every being, and we are all special in God's eyes. We all share the love of God equally.

"Many miracles were attributed to me due to the grace of the Almighty. But despite witnessing those miracles, my brethren were neither repentant nor united when we wandered the deserts. Even I as their leader had a very tough time keeping the flock together. To this day I can vividly recall the burning bush and hear the words of God telling me, 'Moses! Remove your sandals. You are standing on hallowed ground.'

"Prophets and avatars come and go, but humanity continues in its ignorant existence, believing in exclusive rights and superiorities over others. Toward the end of my earthly career, I became very dejected at the behavior of my followers, but the Lord God scolded me for my lack of faith and told me that I might not be the one to take them to the Promised Land but that He had infinite patience and would wait for eternity for them to change their hearts.

"Too much blood has been shed and too many precious lives have been lost. I came here to initiate a movement to stop all of this bloodshed once and for all."

Moses walked back to his seat after this emotional speech and applause resounded around the large auditorium. The Prophet Mohammed, sensing it was his turn, stood up and started speaking.

"Allah ho Akbar! God is great. No amount of praise can adequately describe the glory of the all-knowing, all-powerful and compassionate Allah. I am historically the youngest among my holy brethren here and I consider it a great privilege to speak to all you gathered here. I remember clearly how my own message was received with great hostility when I was driven from Mecca to Medina. No prophet is respected in his own birthplace and what is worse is that he is recognized and adored by millions only after his death.

"When I instituted the zakat (alms giving, one of the five pillars of Islam) and other disciplines, such as praying five times a day, I meant it as an internal spiritual discipline for inner evolution. Islam stands for true compassion and love. This crazy violence and jihad (holy war) that we're witnessing today, as well as the Crusades from centuries ago, were never part of my teachings. The holy war was not to be against any external enemies, but only the inner enemies that lurk in the dark regions of the mind. I thought this message was very clearly embodied in the Holy Koran, the inspiration that I received from God.

"All of us on stage here would be rejected if we were to return to earth today because religions have become hierarchical structures whose only interest is in continuing their false existence of control and mind games. Our messages have become so twisted and warped over the centuries that they are no longer recognizable to us.

"Just look at the countless religious wars throughout human history. War continues as an act of revenge by generations after generations. The fundamental question is not who started it. The more important answer is who will end it? Anyone can perpetuate violence, but it takes a super-human to end violence and sow the seeds of love.

"Love of God and love of other humans cannot be separated from one another. All beings have been created equal and all beings are equal, irrespective of their race, creed, gender, social status, and belief systems. Yet humanity, in spite of its advances in science and technology and worldly comforts, has fallen behind in human values and human compassion.

"I wholeheartedly agree with the speakers before me that something ought to be done differently to change the basic attitudes of all of humanity and help usher them into the golden age."

The Prophet Mohammed finished his speech and everybody stood up cheering him. Finally all eyes turned to Sri Krishna to hear his final remarks.

"Swagatham[49]. Welcome to everyone," said Krishna. "Embodiments of love! Peace be upon you. Representing the oldest religion known to humankind,

---

[49] Swagatham: The word for "warm welcome" in Sanskrit. This word can be split into "swa" + "ghatham," which literally means "you can step in according to your own preferences." True welcome is to give the ultimate freedom to the guest to be as comfortable as he or she is in his or her own home. There is also the inner meaning that you are welcome to cherish your own ambitions, ideals, and aspirations. This has been the goal and practice of Sanathana Dharma of India since the beginning of time. There was never an organized effort by Hindus to convert anyone into their religion in recorded history. The Rig Veda starts with the prayer "Let noble thoughts come from every quarter."

the Sanathana Dharma (Eternal Wisdom), more recently referred to as Hinduism, I stand here speechless at the state of the world today. Every age has had its ups and downs, finest hours and darkest moments.

"The Bhagavad Gita, the Bible, the Torah, the Dhamma Paadhaa, the Koran, the Zend Avestha—no matter what the sacred scripture is called, each proclaims the glory of God and the power of God's love. I have myself declared, 'Whenever there is the rise of evil or the decline of righteousness, I will be born again and again to guide humanity back to its divine origin and blissful coexistence.'

"I shall come again and again, as often as needed to restore faith in humans' hearts. Do not despair. The golden age is not far off. While the current era seems to bear witness to the most violent upheavals in the nature of human beings, it is also a time of transition, as the human race silently knits together, transcending national and political boundaries, cultures and languages. With more exposure to other cultures, one's perspective changes and rises to a new level. The human race is truly coming together as never before. The last challenge to this advancement comes from the entrenched religious structures that have been falsely formed in our names. People are now recognizing their commonality as never before and embracing one another with love and acceptance, which threatens some religious and political leaders who are the last holdouts. These few individuals continue to promote violence, fear, and greed as their weapons of destruction, but soon universal love will render these weapons obsolete as they usher in the golden age.

"Your anxieties are over. This is not the worst of times. This is going to become the best of all times. A divine being fully endowed with all the powers of the Almighty, embodying the power of Supreme Love, is already among the humans. Very soon He will turn sky into earth and earth into sky. He shall establish the Kingdom of God on earth. His name will be Truth . . ."

The excited crowd cheered so loudly that Vivek could not hear the rest of the words spoken by Krishna. There was a mad rush by all those assembled to be close to the divine beings on stage. Vivek watched it all from the back of the auditorium and thought that he was the only one until Chidanandji walked up.

When he came back to consciousness, Vivek was still sitting cross-legged under the branches of the Wish-Fulfilling tree and Chidanandji was urging him to get up. Vivek wanted to ask Chidanandji about Krishna's promise but Chidanandji did not seem to be the a mood talk to him. He silently motioned for Vivek to follow.

Chapter 19

Vivek walked silently behind Chidanandji, lost in his thoughts. He wanted to know whether what he had witnessed was a hallucination of his own imagining or a real experience. After several hours of walking, Vivek recognized the familiar landscape. He could hear the distant roar of the Ganga falling from the cavern above. They were back near the entrance of the Bhageeratha Cave. Chidanandji finally sat on a marble bench and motioned to Vivek to sit beside him.

"Chidanandji, I had an amazing experience under the Wish-Fulfilling Tree," Vivek told him.

"I know," said Chidanandji. "I was there. I was part of your experience."

"Was that real?" Vivek asked.

Chidanandji looked at him. "What do you think?"

"It seemed real," Vivek replied.

"Then it must be real," Chidanandji said.

Vivek was yearning to learn more. "But can I personally talk to Krishna and other great beings?" he asked.

"Well, you did, sort of," Chidanandji replied. "That whole experience was crafted for your sake. You are the divine messenger who is supposed to carry this message to earth."

Vivek objected. "But I heard Krishna say that He is born on earth again."

"Yes, that is true," said Chidanandji.

"So then why am I a messenger if he's already there?" Vivek was still trying to put the puzzle together.

"Because God needs everyone since God is everyone. He has chosen you to be His messenger. You will join Krishna in human form soon to take part in His mission."

"And what is that?" Vivek prodded.

"Your mission is to submit to His Divine Will," Chidanandji responded.

"But I don't have a clue as to where He is on earth or what He is called. I couldn't hear him talk at the end because of the crowd cheering. I must have missed the most important point. But you must know who He is and where He is."

Chidanandji smiled. "You will know when you need to know. Actually, every human being is a messenger of God. Everyone is an angel doing God's work whether he or she acknowledges it or not. Everyone goes through three stages: First you are in the light. Then you discover that the light is within you, and finally you recognize that you are the light.

"Fire is the source, light is the essence, and heat is the effect. Similarly wisdom is the source, love is the essence, and austerity or selfless service is the effect. This is the message embodied in the life of every master, east or west, north or south.

"All powers are within you. Fifty years ago, if someone had seen that a person could instantly talk to another person ten thousand miles away, could instantly see someone on the other side of the globe, and could know what happens thousands of miles away, they would have considered that person to be some kind of deity. Yet scientific fact overrides religious belief with each new advance in wireless technology, satellites, telephones, TVs, and computers. One thing is constant: Science can't evaluate or design and build love, truth, and beauty, which all emanate from God's grace.

"These pale in comparison to our real potential. If we overcome our physical, mental, and intellectual limitations, each one of us can truly become omnipotent, omniscient, and omnipresent in the biblical sense.

"In spite of your worldly ambitions, weaknesses, and failures, you have within you this thirst and urge for universal wisdom and selfless love. That is the reason that you were chosen and why I was asked to bring you here. Now our stay here is almost coming to an end. It is time to go back to earth. But first, will you do something for me?" Chidanandji asked.

"Of course, Chidanandji, I would do anything for you. You've done so much for me that I can never fully repay your kindness."

Chidanandji stared intently into Vivek's eyes before asking him the question. "Give me a solemn promise that from now on, you will love everyone, no matter who they are. You will accept them for who they are, expecting nothing from them. You will offer your love in the fullest measure to anyone and everyone you come across in your life. That is all I ask of you."

With tears welling up in his eyes, Vivek held both of Chidanandji's hands and promised that he would abide by his wishes.

Chidanandji was touched by Vivek's emotional response. "Vivek," he said. "I am touched by your love, humility, and devotion. My earthly sojourn is almost coming to an end. I have to take you back to earth before then and make sure that you are on your way to meet God on earth. Before I leave, I will give you a bunch of sacred leaves from the heavens, which I will request you to offer on my behalf at the feet of the Divine One when you meet Him. I am myself not privileged to see Him in physical from, but you are destined to see Him and be with Him."

With these words Chidanandji wiped away the tears that had started to form and guided Vivek to a secluded spot near the giant waterfalls. The deafening roar of the falls was almost too much for Vivek's ears. Chidanandji guided him through the mist to what seemed like the opening of a small cave.

Chapter 20

Vivek followed Chidanandji through the narrow entrance to the cave close to the waterfall. He could hardly see anything through the thick mist created by the tremendous force of the falls. Suddenly, it became very dark, the sunlight blocked by the massive volume of the water's flow. Vivek held onto Chidanandji's left hand and slowly walked over the gravel and mud floor of the cave. The water had sprayed over from the falls into the cave and it was slushy and muddy in some places. After walking for what seemed like an eternity, they arrived near a larger cavern where sunlight peeped through the opening above.

This was another large cave, a miniature version of the Bhageeratha Ghufa. There was a still pond at the center of the cavern and Vivek could discern some huts on its banks. Chidanandji guided Vivek into an empty hut at the farthest corner of the pond. They were enveloped by an eerie silence; not even the birds or creatures living there seemed to dare to make any noise.

Chidanandji suddenly turned to Vivek and said, "Contact Greg."

That was the last thing that Vivek expected Chidanandji to say. "What? You mean Greg Keaton?" He was confused. "How do I contact Greg from here and also, why now?"

"Don't you remember?" Chidanandji said. "Just before you left the U.S., did you not tell Greg that you would contact him in exactly one month, from wherever you were? Well, today is exactly one month later. See, you have now reached a level of awareness and understanding where the truth of your words is more important than anything else. Anything you say will come true. Your words will heal. Similarly, any words spoken by you in anger or resentment will harm others. From now on, you have to be very careful about what you think, speak, or do. You promised Greg and now you must contact him. Tell him to come with Amanda to Thiruvannamalai in exactly two weeks. We will meet them at Thiruvannamalai."

"Oh, dear," Vivek said. "That may be a problem, since my cell phones is dead and still in Tapovan."

"Don't worry about it." Chidanandji spoke softly, "In this physio-astral world they are of little use to you anyway. Just think of Greg and you will be able to talk to him. He will receive your thoughts as if through a phone call."

Vivek nodded. He thought of Greg, and the instant he did, it seemed the phone rang at Greg's house. "Hello? Who is this?" said Greg.

Vivek continued his transmitting through his thoughts. "This is your conscience speaking."

Greg grew excited as he recognized his friend's voice. "Hey, buddy! Is it really you? Where are you calling from? Tell me what's going on. Just yesterday Amanda called and told me not to worry about you since you were with Chidanandji."

Vivek chuckled to himself. "Greg, even if I told you where I am, you would not believe it. Anyway, the reason I called you is that Chidanandji has a special message for both you and Amanda. He wants you both to come to Thiruvannamalai in two weeks. He said that he and I will meet you there."

"Oh, wow, sure!" Greg was dumbfounded. "I'll call Amanda right away, and please give Chidanandji my respects."

Following the "phone call," Chidanandji told Vivek to calmly sit in the hut and focus on the area between his eyebrows. In an instant Vivek was focusing on the space between his thoughts and like a rocket piercing the skies, he very rapidly transcended the realm of form. Soon he felt he was all alone in an empty space surrounded by distant stars. He could see beings made of light moving around with trails of aura behind them. He was totally absorbed in the sound of "Om," which reverberated everywhere. His perception became finer and finer, until he even transcended the faculty of perception.

Vivek felt that his spirit was a part of all existence. His physical body had already disintegrated into the elements of nature when he entered the Bhageeratha cave. He was now lost in bliss, unaware of space, time, or any other limitation.

When he regained consciousness and opened his eyes, he saw Chidanandji sitting in front of him looking at him with compassion. They did not talk. Chidanandji motioned for Vivek to follow him. They walked together for some time until they reached a secluded section of the giant cavern, where Vivek saw a large cauldron with a huge column of fire towering up toward the roof of the cavern.

Without any warning, Chidanandji commanded Vivek to enter that column of fire. Before Vivek could object or question why, Chidanandji grabbed his hand and pulled him into the fire with him.

Contrary to Vivek's fears, he did not feel the heat or suffer any burns. The fearsome fire felt harmless and he felt exhilarated, as if they were hurtling down the column of fire with tremendous force. As they were falling down, Vivek could see different shades and layers of fire, with the hues ranging from dark brown to dark red to yellow.

He also felt that every one of his body's organs was being regenerated, one atom and one molecule and one cell at a time. He felt as if his entire physical body were being re-created and purified in that holy fire. Finally they both landed on what seemed like hard ground. Since they came down with tremendous force, they both felt dizzy for a while. After a few minutes, Chidanandji got up and asked Vivek to follow him. It felt as if they were inside another huge cavern, but quite unlike the previous one.

They walked again for some time in silence. Vivek wondered what was coming next. He turned around and saw behind him the huge column of fire, whose distant glow was dimly lighting the passageway. The whole cave seemed to be vibrating with the sound of "Om." Chidanandji suddenly pushed a rock aside and slid through a narrow opening. Vivek followed, and he was almost blinded by the sunlight. Though the column of fire inside the cave was a thousand times brighter, it did not blind him or hurt him like the sunlight from the eastern sky of the Thiruvannamalai landscape.

Vivek recognized the area. It was where he had met Chidanandji over a year before. The mud pot was still there but broken. Next to it was Vivek's backpack, which he had left at Tapovan. It had magically traveled all the way from the Himalayas to Thiruvannamalai. Vivek felt light in his body. Chidanandji sat down on a rock and motioned for Vivek to sit down as well.

"Vivek," he said gently. "You have been away from these familiar surroundings and the physical plane of the earth for almost a month. You are also wearing a new body, which needs to adjust to the environment. Take a few slow breaths to acclimate your lungs and blood vessels. You will start feeling hungry, since you have not felt the need to eat anything for almost a month."

Vivek started breathing slowly. "Chidanandji," he said. "I still can't believe what I've gone through. We were near Gomukh just a short while ago and now we are at Thiruvannamalai. How is it possible?"

"First there was space, then fire, air, water, and earth," Chidanandji explained patiently. "The rocks in this Thiruvannamalai Mountain are carbon-dated to three billion years, the age of the solar system, while the rocks in the Himalayan Mountains are only fifty million years old. These two mystic centers are connected in the astral plane. That is why we were able to make the journey.

"As a matter of fact, in our astral and mental form, we can go to any distant galaxy if we wish to do so. Science is not advanced enough to understand these things. The biggest stumbling block for science, as Arametheus pointed out, is the refusal to believe that mind and matter are of the same stuff. You are indeed fortunate to get this unique experience. But this is just the beginning. You are going to experience many more amazing things proclaiming the glory of God and His creation. Let us not waste much time. You are getting hungry and so am I. Let us walk back to the temple and see whether we can get some prasad[50] there."

Together Chidanandji and Vivek hiked back down the mountain and followed the road that had been used for thousands of years. They walked almost six miles and finally reached the entrance of the temple. They washed themselves in the pond and went inside to have darshan. Inside the temple, the priest gave them some prasad in a leaf. They consumed that food like the weary and famished travelers they were.

They had hardly rested when Vivek looked up to see Greg and Amanda entering the courtyard of the temple. He jumped up and yelled. Amanda was dressed in a cotton sari with the red mark symbolizing purity, auspiciousness, and sacrifice on her forehead, like a typical Indian woman. Greg Keaton was dressed in an Indian kurtha and pyjaama. When they heard Vivek yelling, they ran toward him and embraced their friend, their hearts overflowing with love.

---

[50]   Prasad: Sweet rice and lemon rice which has been sanctified as an offering to the deity.

Chapter 21

As the friends hugged and shook hands in the courtyard, Chidanandji sauntered up and joined them. "Saraswathi," he said, referring to Amanda by her name from her previous birth. "I am glad to see you again. Greg, it is a pleasure to finally meet you. Accept my blessings. Saraswathi, tell me how you've been."

Amanda turned to Chidanandji to talk and catch up, and before Vivek could open his mouth to tell Greg anything about his recent experiences, Greg started talking.

"Vivek, you won't believe what happened to me. That day after you left, I had the most unbelievable experience of my life. I was wide awake for a while and then began to doze off in that half-asleep, half-awake state. Suddenly I was awakened by a brilliant light in the room. I saw at the foot of the bed the most beautiful human form I had ever seen. He was a short man with an Afro and an orange robe with a hand raised as if he was blessing. I swear, he looked like he was floating on air at the foot of the bed. He had the most beautiful smile and I could clearly see him beckoning for me to come.

"It lasted several seconds and then he slowly disappeared. I immediately called Amanda to talk about it. She wasn't sure who the being was and then told me about her own past and her relationship with Chidanandji, and how Chidanandji holds you in special affection. Okay, so now it gets even weirder." Vivek smiled, knowing that Greg had not a clue yet as to what weird really was. He listened as his friend continued relating his experience. "The next day, I went to Borders looking for something to read, and as I left the store, I saw a shopping cart with a book in it. I glanced down and about fell over—there was a picture on the cover, and guess what? It was the dude I had seen in my room the night before! I grabbed it and saw that the book was about this mysterious person I'd seen in my vision. I went and tried to return it but was told that they didn't even sell it there and they gave the book back to me. You have to agree, that's too much of a coincidence to be a coincidence.

"So I went back home and read the entire book in one sitting, and I was struck by the power of his simple teachings," Greg said. "What he's saying is really quite remarkable. I wondered if Chidanandji knew this mysterious man or if we were even going to meet him and if that was why Chidanandji asked us to come here." Greg stopped as he looked over and saw Chidanandji smiling at him and Vivek.

"Vivek," Chidanandji said. "You asked me earlier about where you would find the divine incarnation and who that person might be. After hearing about Greg's experience, I'm sure you're even more curious. The truth is that the person from Greg's vision is the one I was summoned to guide you to. Let me tell you a few things about this divine incarnation that has come to earth."

Suddenly Chidanandji's voice became stronger and louder. He became animated as he started talking about this divine phenomenon. Chidanandji said, "This divine being that has manifested on earth has come armed with all the powers of gods. He can transform sky into earth and earth into sky. You will know him this way: His name is truth. He has miraculous powers to transform the lives of the people on earth. He raises the dead and heals the sick. He embraces the tenets of all religions and he respects the founders of all of them. He leads the way to religious unity and spiritual harmony. He teaches by his example. He shows the world that food, education, health care, and basic amenities such as drinking water are the basic rights of every citizen of the world. He embarks on projects such as helping to build hospitals with free medical care for the poor across the world, as well as educational institutions that offer free education. He undertakes mammoth works like bringing drinking water to the masses in dry lands. He utters the highest truth in the simplest manner. He declares categorically that 'I am God and so are you,' and says to all, 'Fill your hearts with peace. Love and serve thy neighbors. Help ever, hurt never.'"

Chidanandji choked with emotion. "I am not destined to see him in person," he said, "but now the time has come for you, Greg, and Amanda to go to his birthplace. All roads lead to his village and all hearts lead to him. Peace be with you."

With that, he raised both of his hands to bless the three of them. A couple of tears rolled down his cheeks. In an instant, he dematerialized. Where he had stood lay his ochre robe, neatly folded. On the robe was a small bouquet of tulsi (sacred basil) leaves tied by a silk thread. Amanda, Greg, and Vivek were too shocked to react. Vivek remembered what Chidanandji had told him at the Bhageeratha Ghufa: that he had only a few more days to live, and that before he was to go, he would give Vivek a bouquet of tulsi leaves to offer at the Lotus Feet of God on earth. Amanda started sobbing at the abrupt separation from her dear friend. Vivek's eyes welled with tears and Greg was speechless for the first time. Vivek picked up the robe and gave it to Amanda. He then picked up the tulsi bouquet, placing it carefully in his backpack.

Suddenly Vivek's thoughts flashed to his parents. He wondered how they would feel about his incredible journey and also about his new quest to find a God on earth. He wondered whether they would approve of his latest adventure. However, there was no more time to speculate about such things.

Soon Vivek, Amanda, and Greg were in a taxi barreling toward an unknown destination, racing to the place where they'd been told God had been incarnated. Vivek didn't know whether to cry at the loss of Chidanandji, whom he might not ever meet again, or smile at the prospect of coming face-to-face with God in human form. As the cool breeze brushed past his cheeks, he closed his eyes in deep contemplation. Who knew what great fortunes lay ahead, waiting to be unveiled?

Glossary

Adi Shankara: A great sage and philosopher who lived a millennium ago. By the age of five he had renounced the world and become a monk. By the age of sixteen he had composed some of the greatest commentaries on Indian scriptures, especially the Bhagavad Gita (Song Celestial), the Brahma Sutra (the Aphorisms on the Absolute) and the Upanishads (the greatest philosophical treatises of India), and his works were referred to as Shankara Bhashya or Shankara's commentary or exposition. He traveled the length and breadth of India four times before he attained Maha Samadhi (Final Emancipation) by the age of 32. He popularized the Advaitha (Nondualism) philosophy and established four mutts (learning centers) at the four corners of India. Many consider him to be an incarnation of Shiva, due to his monumental accomplishments. It is because of Shankara's brilliance that Buddhism and Jainism almost became part of mainstream Hinduism, and only pockets of believers in these religions remain in India after Shankara's advent.

Advaitha: The most abstract and highest form of Hindu philosophy, which propounds the fundamental belief that all of creation consists of the one all-pervasive, eternal, never-changing Atma, or Divine Spirit. According to Advaitha, this phenomenal universe is nothing but an illusion, and the goal and purpose of life for embodied human beings is to realize the absolute oneness with Atma.

Aakaasa : Sky

Ananda: Bliss

Ashram: A hermitage where a guru or spiritual teacher lives with his students. An ashram can also be considered as an in-residence spiritual school.

Atma: Refers to the universal in-dwelling spirit that permeates all of creation just as space permeates all of the physical cosmos. Atma is another name for supreme consciousness.

Badrinaath: Sacred Himalayan temple dedicated to Lord Vishnu, the protector among the trinity of gods.

Bhageerath was a prince who in order to save the lives of his thousands of brothers who were cursed by a sage for inappropriate behavior, did penance for thousands of years to bring the heavenly Ganga down to earth so that when she passed over the ashes of his brothers, they would come back to life. The force of the Ganges on the earth was feared to have devastating consequences, so Bhageerath prayed for another thousand years to Lord Shiva to tame her. When Ganga came with tremendous force, Lord Shiva captured her in the tresses of his hair. Once again Bhageerath prayed for a thousand years to propitiate the grace of Shiva to release her, at which point she was released as a gentle stream, hence the divine origin of Ganaga or Ganges.

Bhakthi Yoga: The path of perfection through purifying the emotions.

Brahma Muhurtham: The early-morning hours between 3:00 and 6:00 a.m. This time is considered auspicious for contemplation.

Chutney: Spicy side dish made from chili and coconut or onion

Cricket: A game played in India and many colonial countries. It is very similar to baseball, but is a game dominated by the hitter, who is called the batsman. The pitcher is called a bowler. Unlike a baseball game, which has low scores, cricket is a high-scoring game and is played not just for hours but for days at a time.

Darshan: The sight or vision of a holy person

Deva Daru: *Cedrus deodara* or the evergreen tree of the Himalayas

Dharma: A common interpretation for this Sanskrit word is "duty" or "responsibility." A deeper and more profound meaning of the word refers to a process by which an individual attains a chosen goal (ultimately, perfection itself) in life. Any act or event which delays, prevents, or derails the progress towards the goal is called adharmic, or against dharma.

Dhothi: A single sheet of cloth, generally white, worn by men as a lower garment in South India

Ganga: The river Ganges, which is worshipped as a goddess

Gangotri: The glacier which is the source of the river Ganges. Gangotri literally means "where the Ganges originates."

Gomukh: The very spot where the Ganges flows out of the Gangotri Glacier. Gomukh means "the face of a cow." In ancient days, the boulders used to look like the face of a cow.

Idlis: Rice cake cooked in steam

Jnana Yoga: The path of perfection through refining the intellect and the intuition.

Kamandalam: Portable water pot

Karaikudi: A town in South India, inhabited by the Chettiar community, which later became a university town.

Karma Yoga: Refers to the yoga of action. The Sanskrit word "yoga" refers to perfection or excellence in chosen path. Karma Yoga is the path of perfection through selfless action.

Kedaarnaath: Sacred Himalayan temple dedicated to Lord Shiva, the destroyer among the trinity of gods.

Krishna: The ninth avatar (Divine Descent) of Vishnu, one of the trinity of Hindu gods who is worshipped as the protector. Sri Krishna, along with Sri Rama, is celebrated as the greatest manifestation of God in human form. They have inspired devotion in the hearts of billions of Hindus for thousands of years. They are both historical figures: Rama was the prince of Ayodhya, and Krishna was the prince of Mathira, and later Dwaraka. The story of Sri Krishna is described in great detail in the epics Maha Bharatha and the Srimad Bhagavatham.

Lakshman Jhula: A swinging bridge across the Ganges in Rishikesh

Lakshmi: Goddess of wealth, consort of Vishnu, one among the trinity who protects the entire creation.

Lokas: The various planes of existence, such as physical, astral, and causal. It is believed that there are 14 such planes of consciousness. Man's physical existence is right in the middle.

Maha Samadhi: The experience of total equanimity while alive. Generally, samadhi is short-lived and is experienced only for a few hours or days. However, Maha Samadhi means the experience of permanent and total equanimity that one experiences after death. A person who has attained Maha Samadhi is never born again.

Nirvikalpa Samaadhi: Final and ultimate cessation of all thoughts once and for all, leading to an everlasting peace. "Nir vikalpa" means no more thought modifications.

Mahatma: Great Soul

Navarathri: Nine nights dedicated to the worship of the Divine Mother

Nirvana: The state of final emancipation from suffering

OM: The symbol of cosmic vibrations, representing the fundamental frequency of creation. Even cosmology talks about a background humming noise of the universe, which may also refer to the Om sound. "Om" is a Sanskrit word which is also pronounced as "aum"—"a" representing the wakeful stage, "u" representing the dream stage, and "m" representing the deep sleep stage, with the silence that follows representing a fourth stage, which is beyond human comprehension.

Raaja Yoga: The path of perfection through fine-tuning the body and the mind.

Ramanaashram: The spiritual hermitage at the famous South Indian town of Thiruvannamalai, a hundred and sixty miles from Chennai. This hermitage was inspired by Ramana Maharishi (Great Sage) who lived sixty years ago and revived the path of wisdom by popularizing the enquiry path of asking "Who am I?"

Rishikesh: The sacred valley just before the Ganges enters the plains of India. In Sanskrit, this word means "the place where one can master the senses."

Roti: Flat wheat bread

Samaadhi: A mind totally absorbed in its chosen ideal, experiencing total equanimity

Saambhar: A spicy lentil-soup-like dish

Sanyasis: Renunciants who have dedicated their lives in pursuit of God realization

Sat: Existence

Satsang: A group activity in which spiritual wisdom is shared between spiritual aspirants, or between a teacher and his pupils. Bible study or a church sermon are typical examples. The true meaning of satsang, however, is "sat" (truth) and "sang" (companionship), namely companionship with truth or with one's own real essence.

Savasana: A yogic posture in which a person lies flat on the floor or bed as if he were dead, totally relaxing all the limbs of the body.

Savikalpa Samaadhi: Total absorption of the mind into a single idea, concept or form of an object to the exclusion of everything else. The mind is temporarily suspended from all mental activities.

Shiva: The God of destruction among the trinity of Hindu gods

Shivaling Peak: The glacier mountain that resembles a Shivalinga, an oval-shaped stone, a symbol of the formless God.

Somalata: A legendary plant that grows in the heights of the Himalayan Mountains and is well known for its ability to promote longevity and the rejuvenation of the physical body.

Sri Nagar: Capital city of Kashmir

Swaagatham: The word for "warm welcome" in Sanskrit. This word can be split into "swa" + "ghatham," which literally means "you can step in according to your own preferences." True welcome is to give the ultimate freedom to the guest to be as comfortable as he or she is in his or her own home. There is also the inner meaning that you are welcome to cherish your own ambitions, ideals, and aspirations. This has been the goal and practice of Sanathana Dharma of India since the beginning of time. There was never an organized effort by Hindus to convert anyone into their religion in recorded history. The Rig Veda starts with the prayer "Let noble thoughts come from every quarter."

Swarga: Sanskrit word for Heaven

Taj Hotel: A chain of five-star hotels primarily in India and abroad

Uttar Kashi: A sacred city in the Himalayan ranges en route to Gangotri, the source of Ganges. The term literally means "North Kashi," in reference to Kashi, the most sacred city in India (also called Varanasi or Benares), on the banks of Ganges.

Vasana: Refers to the subtlest form of desire deeply buried within. It is believed that after death, the predominant desires of man are stored as vasanas in the Karana Sareera, or causal body. Until the vasanas are completely exhausted or fulfilled, humans take repeated births to enjoy the consequences of their previous actions. The total cessation of vasanas is called Moksha, or liberation.

Vaishaak Poornima: The full-moon day in the month of Vaishak in the Hindu lunar calendar

Vaishnavi Devi Temple: Temple of Mother Goddess in Kashmir near Sri Nagar

Vibhudhi: Sacred ash to be worn on the forehead or smeared over the body as a symbol of renunciation as well as a symbol of the unreality of the phenomenal universe. Since ash cannot be further transformed into something else, it is supposed to represent the ultimate immutable and unchangeable reality.

Yamunotri: The source of the river Yamuna

Edwards Brothers,Inc!
Thorofare, NJ 08086
30 November, 2010
BA2010335